W9-AMN-915

RON KOVIC'S TERRIBLE TRAGEDY IS
AMERICA'S . . . AND IT HAS NEVER
BEEN WRITTEN "WITH MORE FORCE
AND FEELING!"

—*Los Angeles Times*

BORN ON THE FOURTH OF JULY

A SEARINGLY REALISTIC ACCOUNT written in
red-hot prose . . . the most powerful book on the
Vietnam war yet to be published."

—*John Barkham Reviews*

"An important book . . . bound to affect people . . .
both enthralling and dangerous."

—*Bookletter*

"Ron Kovic has returned from the dead and given us
an honest, unrefined account of his struggle."

—*The Washington Post*

"Tears you to pieces . . . everyone ought to read it!"

—*Kansas City Star*

"This book will make you cry . . ."

—*Pittsburgh Press*

"EXTRAORDINARILY EFFECTIVE . . . KOVIC'S
UNABASHED EXPRESSION OF FEELINGS . . .
BECOMES A FORM OF BRAVERY."

—*Newsweek*

BORN ON THE FOURTH OF JULY

RON KOVIC

POCKET BOOKS

New York London Toronto Sydney Tokyo Singapore

POCKET BOOKS, a division of Simon & Schuster Inc.
1230 Avenue of the Americas, New York, NY 10020

Published by arrangement with McGraw-Hill Book Company
Library of Congress Catalog Card Number: 76-7508

ISBN 0-671-68149-4

First Pocket Books printing July 1977

18 17 16 15

ACKNOWLEDGMENTS

First, I'd like to thank my friend and editor, Joyce Johnson, for the countless hours, including much of her own time, spent helping construct this book, giving it the necessary shape and form. The book could not have been completed without her help and exceptional skills and talents.

Thanks also to Roger Steffens—actor, poetry-man, and friend—who gave freely of his time, effort, and energy, retyping almost the entire manuscript up in Mendocino. I'll remember his patience and understanding, his generosity and love, his faith in me and the book.

I'd also like to thank Mary and Sheila and my friend Waldo—a child at sixty—who gave me courage with his eyes and love with his wisdom.

And finally, thanks to Connie Panzarino—beautiful, strong, and brave woman—who believed in me and the book years before it had been written. She stood by me like no one else, listening through nights and days, caring and loving, understanding and encouraging, wiping the tears from my eyes. She was like a light shining from the darkness of what seemed to be an endless storm.

For my country
and its people,

happy birthday

Ask not what your country can do for you—ask what you can do for your country.

—President John F. Kennedy
   January 20, 1961

I am the living death
the memorial day on wheels
I am your yankee doodle dandy
your john wayne come home
your fourth of july firecracker
exploding in the grave

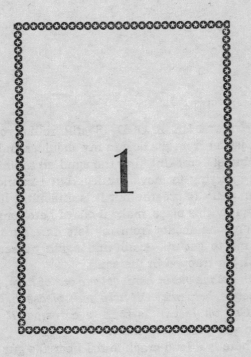

1

THE BLOOD IS still rolling off my flak jacket from the hole in my shoulder and there are bullets cracking into the sand all around me. I keep trying to move my legs but I cannot feel them. I try to breathe but it is difficult. I have to get out of this place, make it out of here somehow.

Someone shouts from my left now, screaming for me to get up. Again and again he screams, but I am trapped in the sand.

Oh get me out of here, get me out of here, please someone help me! Oh help me, please help me. Oh God oh Jesus! "Is there a corpsman?" I cry. "Can you get a corpsman?"

There is a loud crack and I hear the guy begin to sob. "They've shot my fucking finger off! Let's go, sarge! Let's get outta here!"

"I can't move," I gasp. "I can't move my legs! I can't feel anything!"

I watch him go running back to the tree line.

"Sarge, are you all right?" Someone else is calling to me now and I try to turn around. Again there is the sudden crack of a bullet and a boy's voice crying. "Oh Jesus! Oh Jesus Christ!" I hear his body fall in back of me.

I think he must be dead but I feel nothing for him, I just want to live. I feel nothing.

And now I hear another man coming up from behind, trying to save me. "Get outta here!" I scream. "Get the fuck outta here!"

A tall black man with long skinny arms and enormous hands picks me up and throws me over his shoulder as bullets begin cracking over our heads like strings of firecrackers. Again and again they crack as the sky swirls around us like a cyclone. "Motherfuckers motherfuckers!" he screams. And the rounds keep cracking and the sky and the sun on my face and my body all gone, all twisted up dangling like a puppet's, diving again and again into the sand, up and down, rolling and cursing, gasping for breath. "Goddamn goddamn motherfuckers!"

And finally I am dragged into a hole in the sand with the bottom of my body that can no longer feel, twisted and bent underneath me. The black man runs from the hole without ever saying a thing. I never see his face. I will never know who he is. He is gone. And others now are in the hole helping me. They are bandaging my wounds. There is fear in their faces.

"It's all right," I say to them. "Everything is fine."

Someone has just saved my life. My rifle is gone and I don't feel like finding it or picking it up ever again. The only thing I can think of, the only thing that crosses my mind, is living. There seems to be nothing in the world more important than that.

Hundreds of rounds begin to crash in now. I stare up at the sky because I cannot move. Above the hole men are running around in every direction. I see their legs and frightened faces. They are screaming and dragging the wounded past me. Again and again the rounds crash in. They seem to be coming in closer and closer. A tall man jumps in, hugging me to the earth.

"Oh God!" he is crying. "Oh God please help us!"

The attack is lifted. They are carrying me out of the hole now—two, three, four men—quickly they are strapping me to a stretcher. My legs dangle off the sides until they realize I cannot control them. "I can't move them," I say, almost in a whisper. "I can't move them." I'm still carefully sucking the air, trying to calm myself, trying not to get excited, not to panic. I want to live. I keep telling myself, Take it slow now, as they strap my legs to the stretcher and carry my wounded body into an Amtrac packed with other wounded men. The steel trapdoor of the Amtrac slowly closes as we begin to move to the northern bank and back across the river to the battalion area.

Men are screaming all around me. "Oh God get me out of here!" "Please help!" they scream. Oh Jesus, like little children now, not like marines, not like the posters, not like that day in the high school, this is for real. "Mother!" screams a man without a face. "Oh I don't want to die!" screams a young boy cupping his intestines with his hands. "Oh please, oh no, oh God, oh help! Mother!" he screams again.

We are moving slowly through the water, the Amtrac rocking back and forth. We cannot be brave anymore, there is no reason. It means nothing now. We hold on to ourselves, to things around us, to memories, to thoughts, to dreams. I breathe slowly, desperately trying to stay awake.

The steel trapdoor is opening. I see faces. Corpsmen, I think. Others, curious, looking in at us. Air, fresh, I feel, I smell. They are carrying me out now. Over wounded bodies, past wounded screams. I'm in a helicopter now lifting above the battalion area. I'm leaving the war. I'm going to live. I am still breathing, I keep thinking over and over, I'm going to live and get out of here.

They are shoving tubes and needles in my arms. Now we are being packed into planes. I begin to believe more and more as I watch the other wounded packed around me on shelves that I am going to live.

I still fight desperately to stay awake. I am in an ambulance now rushing to some place. There is a man without any legs screaming in pain, moaning like a little baby. He is bleeding terribly from the stumps that were once his legs, thrashing his arms wildly about his chest, in a semiconscious daze. It is almost too much for me to watch.

I cannot take much more of this. I must be knocked out soon, before I lose my mind. I've seen too much today, I think. But I hold on, sucking the air. I shout then curse for him to be quiet.

"My wound is much worse than yours!" I scream. "You're lucky," I shout, staring him in the eyes. "I can feel nothing from my chest down. You at least still have part of your legs. Shut up!" I scream again. "Shut the fuck up, you goddamned baby!" He keeps thrashing his arms wildly above his head and kicking his bleeding stumps toward the roof of the ambulance.

The journey seems to take a very long time, but soon we are at the place where the wounded are sent. I feel a tremendous exhilaration inside me. I have made it this far. I have actually made it this far without giving up and now I am in a hospital where they will operate on me and find out why I cannot feel anything from my chest down anymore. I know I am going to make it now. I am going to make it not because of any god, or any religion, but because *I* want to make it, *I* want to live. And I leave the screaming man without legs and am brought to a room that is very bright.

"What's your name?" the voice shouts.

"Wh-wh-what?" I say.

"What's your name?" the voice says again.

"K-K-Kovic," I say.

"No!" says the voice. "I want your name, rank, and service number. Your date of birth, the name of your father and mother."

"Kovic. Sergeant. Two-oh-three-oh-two-six-one, uh, when are you going to . . ."

"Date of birth!" the voice shouts.

"July fourth, nineteen forty-six. I was born on the Fourth of July. I can't feel . . ."

"What religion are you?"

"Catholic," I say.

"What outfit did you come from?"

"What's going on? When are you going to operate?" I say.

"The doctors will operate," he says. "Don't worry," he says confidently. "They are very busy and there are many wounded but they will take care of you soon."

He continues to stand almost at attention in front of me with a long clipboard in his hand, jotting down all the information he can. I cannot understand why they are taking so long to operate. There is something very wrong with me, I think, and they must operate as quickly as possible. The man with the clipboard walks out of the room. He will send the priest in soon.

I lie in the room alone staring at the walls, still sucking the air, determined to live more than ever now.

The priest seems to appear suddenly above my head. With his fingers he is gently touching my forehead, rubbing it slowly and softly. "How are you," he says.

"I'm fine, Father." His face is very tired but it is not frightened. He is almost at ease, as if what he is doing he has done many times before.

"I have come to give you the Last Rites, my son."

"I'm ready, Father," I say.

And he prays, rubbing oils on my face and placing the crucifix to my lips. "I will pray for you," he says.

"When will they operate?" I say to the priest.

"I do not know," he says. "The doctors are very busy. There are many wounded. There is not much time for anything here but trying to live. So you must try to live my son, and I will pray for you."

Soon after that I am taken to a long room where there are many doctors and nurses. They move quickly around me. They are acting very competent. "You will be fine," says one nurse calmly.

"Breathe deeply into the mask," the doctor says.

"Are you going to operate?" I ask.

"Yes. Now breathe deeply into the mask." As the darkness of the mask slowly covers my face I pray with all my being that I will live through this operation and see the light of day once again. I want to live so much. And even before I go to sleep with the blackness still swirling around my head and the numbness of sleep, I begin to fight as I have never fought before in my life.

I awake to the screams of other men around me. I have made it. I think that maybe the wound is my punishment for killing the corporal and the children. That now everything is okay and the score is evened up. And now I am packed in this place with the others who have been wounded like myself, strapped onto a strange circular bed. I feel tubes going into my nose and hear the clanking, pumping sound of a machine. I still cannot feel any of my body but I know I am alive. I feel a terrible pain in my chest. My body is so cold. It has never been this weak. It feels so tired and out of touch, so lost and in pain. I can still barely breathe. I look around me, at people moving in shadows of numbness. There is the man who had been in the ambulance with me, screaming louder than ever, kicking his bloody stumps in the air, crying for his mother, crying for his morphine.

Directly across from me there is a Korean who has not even been in the war at all. The nurse says he was going to buy a newspaper when he stepped on a booby trap and it blew off both his legs and his arm. And all that is left now is this slab of meat swinging one arm crazily in the air, moaning like an animal gasping for its last bit of life, knowing that death is rushing toward him. The Korean is screaming like a madman at the top of his lungs. I cannot wait for the shots of morphine. Oh, the morphine feels so good. It makes everything dark and quiet. I can rest. I can leave this madness. I can dream of my back yard once again.

When I wake they are screaming still and the lights are on and the clock, the clock on the wall, I can hear it ticking to the sound of their screams. I can hear the dead being carted out and the new wounded being brought in to the beds all around me. I have to get out of this place.

"Can I call you by your first name?" I say to the nurse.

"No. My name is Lieutenant Wiecker."

"Please, can I . . ."

"No," she says. "It's against regulations."

I'm sleeping now. The lights are flashing. The black pilot is next to me. He says nothing. He stares at the ceiling all day long. He does nothing but that. But something is happening now, something is going wrong over there. The nurse is shouting for the machine, and the corpsman is crawling on the black man's chest, he has his knees on his chest and he's pounding it with his fists again and again.

"His heart has stopped!" screams the nurse.

Pounding, pounding, he's pounding his fist into his chest. "Get the machine!" screams the corpsman.

The nurse is pulling the machine across the hangar floor as quickly as she can now. They are trying to put curtains around the whole thing, but the curtains keep slipping and falling down. Everyone, all the wounded who can still see and think, now watch what is happening to the pilot, and it is happening right next to me. The doctor hands the corpsman a syringe, they are laughing as the corpsman drives the syringe into the pilot's chest like a knife. They are talking about the Green Bay Packers and the corpsman is driving his fist into the black man's chest again and again until the black pilot's body begins to bloat up, until it doesn't look like a body at all anymore. His face is all puffy like a balloon and saliva rolls slowly from the sides of his mouth. He keeps staring at the ceiling and saying nothing. "The machine! The machine!" screams the doctor, now climbing on top of the bed, taking the corpsman's place. "Turn on the machine!" screams the doctor.

He grabs a long suction cup that is attached to the machine and places it carefully against the black man's chest. The black man's body jumps up from the bed almost arcing into the air from each bolt of electricity, jolting and arcing, bloating up more and more.

"I'll bet on the Packers," says the corpsman.

"Green Bay doesn't have a chance," the doctor says, laughing.

The nurse is smiling now, making fun of both the doctor and the corpsman. "I don't understand football," she says.

They are pulling the sheet over the head of the black man and strapping him onto the gurney. He is taken out of the ward.

The Korean civilian is still screaming and there is a baby now at the end of the ward. The nurse says it has been napalmed by our own jets. I cannot see the baby but it screams all the time like the Korean and the young man without any legs I had met in the ambulance.

I can hear a radio. It is the Armed Forces radio. The corpsman is telling the baby to shut the hell up and there is a young kid with half his head blown away. They have brought him in and put him where the black pilot has just died, right next to me. He has thick bandages wrapped all around his head till I can hardly see his face at all. He is like a vegetable—a nineteen-year-old vegetable, thrashing his arms back and forth, babbling and pissing in his clean white sheets.

"Quit pissin' in your sheets!" screams the corpsman. But the nineteen-year-old kid who doesn't have any brains anymore makes the corpsman very angry. He just keeps pissing in the sheets and crying like a little baby.

There is a Green Beret sergeant calling for his mother. Every night now I hear him. He has spinal meningitis. He will be dead before this evening is over.

The Korean civilian does not moan anymore. He does not wave his one arm and two fingers above his head. He is dead and they have taken him away too.

There is a nun who comes through the ward now with apples for the wounded and rosary beads. She is very pleasant and smiles at all of the wounded. The corpsman is reading a comic-book, still cursing at the baby. The baby is screaming and the Armed Forces radio is saying that troops will be home soon. The kid with the bloody stumps is getting a morphine shot.

There is a general walking down the aisles now, going to each bed. He's marching down the aisles, marching and facing each wounded man in his bed. A skinny private with a Polaroid camera follows directly behind him. The general is dressed in an immaculate uniform with shiny shoes. "Good afternoon, marine," the general says. "In the name of the President of the United States and the United States Marine Corps, I am proud to present you with the Purple Heart, and a picture," the general says. Just then the skinny man with the Polaroid camera jumps up, flashing a picture of the wounded man. "And a picture to send to your folks."

He comes up to my bed and says exactly the

same thing he has said to all the rest. The skinny man jumps up, snapping a picture of the general handing the Purple Heart to me. "And here," says the general, "here is a picture to send home to your folks." The general makes a sharp left face. He is marching to the bed next to me where the nineteen-year-old kid is still pissing in his pants, babbling like a little baby.

"In the name of the President of the United States," the general says. The kid is screaming now almost tearing the bandages off his head, exposing the parts of his brain that are still left. ". . . I present you with the Purple Heart. And here," the general says, handing the medal to the nineteen-year-old vegetable, the skinny guy jumping up and snapping a picture, "here is a picture . . . ," the general says, looking at the picture the skinny guy has just pulled out of the camera. The kid is still pissing in his white sheets. ". . . And here is a picture to send home. . . ." The general does not finish what he is saying. He stares at the nineteen-year-old for what seems a long time. He hands the picture back to his photographer and as sharply as before marches to the next bed.

"Good afternoon, marine," he says.

The kid is still pissing in his clean white sheets when the general walks out of the room.

I am in this place for seven days and seven nights. I write notes on scraps of paper telling myself over and over that I will make it out of here, that I am going to live. I am squeezing rubber balls with my hands to try to get strong again. I write letters home to Mom and Dad. I dictate them to a woman named Lucy who is with the USO. I am telling Mom and Dad that I am hurt pretty bad but I have done it for America and that it is worth it. I tell them not to worry. I will be home soon.

The day I am supposed to leave has come. I am strapped in a long frame and taken from the place of the wounded. I am moved from hangar to hangar, then finally put on a plane, and I leave Vietnam forever.

2

THE BUS TURNED off a side street and onto the parkway, then into Queens where the hospital was. For the first time on the whole trip everyone was laughing and joking. He felt himself begin to wake up out of the nightmare. This whole area was home to him—the streets, the parkway, he knew them like the back of his hand. The air was fresh and cold and the bus rocked back and forth. "This bus sucks!" yelled a kid. "Can't you guys do any better than this? I want my mother, I want my mother."

The pain twisted into his back, but he laughed with the rest of them—the warriors, the wounded, entering the gates of St. Albans Naval Hospital. The guard waved them in and the bus stopped. He was the last of the men to be taken off the bus. They had to carry him off. He got the impression that he was quite an oddity in his steel frame, crammed inside it like a flattened pancake.

They put him on the neuro ward. It was sterile and quiet. I'm with the vegetables again, he thought. It took a long while to get hold of a nurse. He told her that if they didn't get the top of the frame off his back he would start screaming. They took it off him and moved him back downstairs to another ward. This was a ward for men with open wounds. They put him there because of his heel, which had been all smashed by the first bullet, the back of it blown completely out.

He was now in Ward 1-C with fifty other men who had all been recently wounded in the war—twenty-year-old blind men and amputees, men without intestines, men who limped, men who were in wheelchairs, men in pain. He noticed they all had strange smiles on their faces and he had one too, he thought. They were men who had played with death and cheated it at a very young age.

He lay back in his bed and watched everything happen all around him. He went to therapy every day and worked very hard lifting weights. He had to build up the top of his body if he was ever going to walk again. In Da Nang the doctors had told him to get used to the idea that he would have to sit in a wheelchair for the rest of his life. He had accepted it, but more and more he was dreaming and thinking about walking. He prayed every night after the visitors left. He closed his eyes and dreamed of being on his feet again.

Sometimes the American Legion group from his town came in to see him, the men and their wives and their pretty daughters. They would all surround him in his bed. It would seem to him that he was always having to cheer them up more than they were cheering him. They told him he was a hero and that all of Massapequa was proud of him. One time the commander stood up and said they were even thinking of naming a street after him. But the guy's wife was embarrassed and made her husband shut up. She told him the commander was kidding—he tended to get carried away after a couple of beers.

After he had been in the hospital a couple of weeks, a man appeared one morning and handed him a large envelope. He waited until the man had gone to open it up. Inside was a citation and a medal for Conspicuous Service to the State of New York. The citation was signed by Governor Rockefeller. He stuck the envelope and all the stuff in it under his pillow.

None of the men on the wards were civilian yet, so they had reveille at six o'clock in the morning. All the wounded who could get on their feet were made to stand in front of their beds while a roll call was taken. After roll call they all had to make their beds and do a general clean-up of the entire ward—everything from scrubbing the floors to cleaning the windows. Even the amputees had to do it. No one ever bothered him, though. He usually slept through the whole thing.

Later it would be time for medication, and afterward one of the corpsmen would put him in a wheelchair and push him to the shower room. The corpsman would leave him alone for about five minutes, then pick his body up, putting him on a wooden bench, his legs dangling, his toes barely touching the floor. He would sit in the shower like that every morning watching his legs become smaller and smaller, until after a month the muscle tone had all but disappeared. With despair and frustration he watched his once strong twenty-one-year-old body become crippled and disfigured. He was just beginning to understand the nature of his wound. He knew now it was the worst he could have received without dying or becoming a vegetable.

More and more he thought about what a priest had said to him in Da Nang: "Your fight is just beginning. Sometimes no one will want to hear what you're going through. You are going to have to learn to carry a great burden and most of your learning will be done alone. Don't feel frightened when they leave you. I'm sure you will come through it all okay."

I AM IN a new hospital now. Things are very different than in the last place. It is quiet in the early morning. There is no reveille here. The sun is just beginning to come in through the windows and I can hear the steady dripping of the big plastic bags that overflow with urine onto the floor. The aide comes in the room, a big black woman. She goes to Willey's bed across from me, almost stepping in the puddle of urine. She takes the cork out of the metal thing in his neck and sticks a long rubber tube in, then clicks on the machine by the bed. There is a loud sucking slurping sound. She moves the rubber tube around and around until it sucks all the stuff out of his lungs. After she is done she puts the cork back in his throat and leaves the room.

There are people talking down at the end of the hall. The night shift is getting ready to go home. They are laughing very loud and flushing the toilets, cursing and telling jokes, black men in white uniforms walking past my door. I shut my eyes. I try to get back into the dream I was having.

She is so pretty, so warm and naked lying next to me. She kisses me and begins to unbutton my hospital shirt. "I love you," I hear her say. "I love you." I open my eyes. Something strange is tickling my nose.

It is Tommy the enema man and today is my day to get my enema. "Hey Kovic," Tommy is saying. "Hey Kovic, wake up, I got an enema for you."

She kisses my lips softly at first, then puts her tongue into my mouth. I am running my hands through her hair and she tells me that she loves that. She is unbuttoning my trousers now and her hand is working itself deep down into my pants. I keep driving my tongue into her more furiously than ever. We have just been dancing on the floor, I was dancing very funny like a man on stilts, but now we are making love and just above me I hear a voice trying to wake me again.

"Kovic! I have an enema for you. Come on. We gotta get you outta here."

I feel myself being lifted. Tommy and another aide, a young black woman, picked me up, carefully unhooking my tube. They put my body into the frame, tying my legs down with long white twisted sheets. They lay another big sheet over me. The frame has a long metal bar that goes above my head. My rear end sticks out of a slit that I lie on.

"Okay," shouts Tommy in his gravel voice. "This one's ready to go."

The aide pushes me into the line-up in the hallway. There are frames all over the place now, lined up in front of the blue room for their enemas. It is the Six o'Clock Special. There are maybe twenty guys waiting by now. It looks like a long train, a long assembly line of broken, twisted bodies waiting for deliverance. It is very depressing, all these bodies, half of them asleep, tied down to their frames with their rear ends sticking out. All these bodies bloated, waiting to be released. Every third day I go for my enema and wait with the long line of men shoved against the green hospital wall. I watch the dead bodies being pushed into the enema room, then finally myself.

It is a small blue room and they cram us into it like sardines. Tommy runs back and forth placing the bedpans under our rear ends, laughing and joking, a cigarette dangling from the corner of his mouth. "Okay, okay, let's go!" he shouts. There is a big can of soapy water above each man's head and a tube that comes down from it. Tommy is jumping all around and whistling like a little kid, running to each body, sticking the rubber tubes up into them. He is jangling the pans, undoing little clips on the rubber tubes and filling the bellies up with soapy water. Everyone is trying to sleep, refusing to admit that this whole thing is happening to them. A couple of the bodies in the frames have small radios close to their ears. Tommy keeps running from one frame to the other, changing the rubber gloves on his hands and squirting the tube of lubricant onto his fingers, ramming his hands up into the rear ends, checking each of the bodies out, undoing the little clips. The aide keeps grabbing the bedpans and emptying all the shit into the garbage cans, occasionally missing and splattering the stuff on the floor. She places the empty pans in a machine and closes it up. There is a steam sound and the machine opens with all the bedpans as clean as new.

Oh God, what is happening to me? What is going on here? I want to get out of this place! All these broken men are very depressing, all these bodies so emaciated and twisted in these bedsheets. This is a nightmare. This isn't like the poster down by the post office where the guy stood with the shiny shoes; this is a concentration camp. It is like the pictures of all the Jews that I have seen. This is as horrible as that. I want to scream. I want to yell and tell them that I want out of this. All of this, all these people, this place, these sounds, I want out of this forever. I am only twenty-one and there is still so much ahead of me, there is so much ahead of me.

I am wiped clean and pushed past the garbage cans. The stench is terrible. I try to breathe through my mouth but I can't. I'm trapped. I have to watch, I have to smell. I think the war has made me a little mad—the dead corporal from Georgia, the old man that was shot in the village with his brains hanging out. But it is the living deaths I am breathing and smelling now, the living deaths, the bodies broken in the same war that I have come from.

I am outside now in the narrow hallway. The young black woman is pushing my frame past all the other steel contraptions. I look at her face

for a moment, at her eyes, as she pushes my
frame up against another. I can hear the splashing of water next door in the shower room. The
sun has come up in the Bronx and people are
walking through the hallways. They can look into
all the rooms and see the men through the curtains that never close. It is as if we are a bunch
of cattle, as if we do not really count anymore.

They push me into the shower. The black
woman takes a green plastic container and squirts
it, making a long thin white line from my head
to my legs. She is turning on the water, and after
making sure it is not too hot she hoses me down.

It's like a car wash, I think, it's just like a big
car wash, and I am being pushed and shoved
through with the rest of them. I am being checked
out by Tommy and hosed off by the woman. It is
all such a neat, quick process. It is an incredible
thing to run twenty men through a place like this,
to clean out the bodies of twenty paralyzed men,
twenty bloated twisted men. It is an incredible
feat, a stupendous accomplishment, and Tommy
is a master. Now the black woman is drying me
off with a big white towel and shoving me back
into the hallway.

Oh get me back into the room, get me back
away from these people who are walking by me
and making believe like all the rest that they don't
know what's happening here, that they can't figure out that this whole thing is crazy. Oh God, oh
God help me, help me understand this place.
There goes the nurse and she's running down the
hall, hitting the rubber mat that throws open the

big green metal door with the little windows with the wire in them. Oh nurse please help me nurse, my stomach is beginning to hurt again like it does every time I come out of this place and my head is throbbing, pounding like a drum. I want to get out of this hall where all of you are walking past me. I want to get back into my bed where I can make believe this never happened. I want to go to sleep and forget I ever got up this morning.

I never tell my family when they come to visit about the enema room. I do not tell them what I do every morning with the plastic glove, or about the catheter and the tube in my penis, or the fact that I can't ever make it hard again. I hide all that from them and talk about the other, more pleasant things, the things they want to hear. I ask Mom to bring me *Sunrise at Campobello*, the play about the life of Franklin Roosevelt—the great crisis he had gone through when he had been stricken with polio and the comeback he had made, becoming governor, then president of the United States. There are things I am going through here that I know she will never understand.

I feel like a big clumsy puppet with all his strings cut. I learn to balance and twist in the chair so no one can tell how much of me does not feel or move anymore. I find it easy to hide from most of them what I am going through. All of us are like this. No one wants too many people to know how much of him has really died in the war.

At first I felt that the wound was very interesting. I saw it almost as an adventure. But now it is not an adventure any longer. I see it more and more as a terrible thing that I will have to live with for the rest of my life. Nobody wants to know that I can't fuck anymore. I will never go up to them and tell them I have this big yellow rubber thing sticking in my penis, attached to the rubber bag on the side of my leg. I am afraid of letting them know how lonely and scared I have become thinking about this wound. It is like some kind of numb twilight zone to me. I am angry and want to kill everyone—all the volunteers and the priests and the pretty girls with the tight short skirts. I am twenty-one and the whole thing is shot, done forever. There is no real healing left anymore, everything that is going to heal has healed already and now I am left with the corpse, the living dead man, the man with the numb legs, the man in the wheelchair, the Easter Seal boy, the cripple, the sexlessman, the sexlessman, the man with the numb dick, the man who can't make children, the man who can't stand, the man who can't walk, the angry lonely man, the bitter man with the nightmares, the murder man, the man who cries in the shower.

In one big bang they have taken it all from me, in one clean sweep, and now I am in this place around all the others like me, and though I keep trying not to feel sorry for myself, I want to cry. There is no shortcut around this thing. It is too soon to die even for a man who has died once already.

I try to keep telling myself it is good to still be alive, to be back home. I remember thinking on the ambulance ride to the hospital that this was the Bronx, the place where Yankee Stadium was, where Mickey Mantle played. I think I realized then also that my feet would never touch the stadium grass, ever again; I would never play a game in that place.

The wards are filthy. The men in my room throw their breadcrumbs under the radiator to keep the rats from chewing on our numb legs during the nights. We tuck our bodies in with the sheets wrapped around us. There are never enough aides to go around on the wards, and constantly there is complaining by the men. The most severely injured are totally dependent on the aides to turn them. They suffer the most and break down with sores. These are the voices that can be heard screaming in the night for help that never comes. Urine bags are constantly overflowing onto the floors while the aides play poker on the toilet bowls in the enema room. The sheets are never changed enough and many of the men stink from not being properly bathed. It never makes any sense to us how the government can keep asking money for weapons and leave us lying in our own filth.

Briggs throws his bread over the radiator.

"There he goes again," says Garcia. "That goddamn rat's been there for the last two months."

Briggs keeps the rats in our room well fed. "It's a lot better than having the bastards nibble at your toes during the night," he says with a crazy laugh.

The nurse comes in and Garcia is getting real excited. "I think I pissed in my pants again," he cries. "Mrs. Waters, I think I pissed in my pants."

"Oh Garcia," the pretty nurse scolds, "don't say *piss*, say *urine*. *Urine* is much nicer."

Garcia tells her he is sorry and will call it urine from here on out.

Willey is clicking his tongue again and the nurse goes over to see. "What do you want?" she says to Willey. He is the most wounded of us all. He has lost everything from the neck down. He has lost even more than me. He is just a head. The war has taken everything.

He clicks three times. The nurse knows he wants the stuff sucked out of his lungs, so she does it. Garcia's radio is playing in the background. She slurps all of the stuff out, then walks out of the room. Now Briggs is getting the whiskey bottle out of his top drawer, taking big gulps and cursing out the rats that are still running under the radiator.

Someone please help me understand this thing, this terrible thing that's happening to me. I'm a brave man and I want to be brave even with this wound. I want to understand how I can live with it and with everything else that happened over there, the dead corporal from Georgia and all the other crazy things.

I find a place on the side of the hospital where the old men sit. The grass is very green and they feed the birds from their wheelchairs. They are the old men from the First World War, I am sure of that, and I sit next to them and feed the birds too. I just want to slow down, the whole thing has been moving much too fast, like some wild spinning top, and now I am trying to catch my breath, I am trying to figure out what this whole terrible thing is about.

I read the paper every morning and it always says the war is going on and the president is sending more troops, and I still tell people, whoever asks me, that I believe in the war. Didn't I prove it by going back a second time? I look them all right in the eye and tell them that we are winning and the boys' morale is high. But more and more what I tell them and what I am feeling are becoming two different things. I feel them tearing, tearing at my whole being, and I don't want to talk about the war anymore. I feed the birds and the squirrels. I want things to be simple again, things are just too confusing. The hospital is like the whole war all over again.

The aides, the big tall black guys who spit and sit on the toilet bowls all night, they're doing it again, they're picking up the paralyzed drunks from the hallways, they're wheeling them along the halls to the rooms. Now I see them strapping the men into big lifts, hoisting the drunken bodies back into their beds. And the aides are laughing, they're always laughing the way people laugh at a sideshow, it's all pretty funny to them. We are like a show of puppets dancing on strings for them, dancing to maddening music. They're wheeling all the guys in from the halls because it's late and it's time for all of the bodies to be put back into the beds, for all the tubes to be hooked up, and the drip of the piss bags to start all over again.

There's a train in the Bronx, somewhere out over the Harlem River, and it sounds so good, it sounds warm and wonderful like the heater back home, like the Long Island train that I used to hear as a kid. Pat, the new guy, is crying for help. He's puking into the cup again and he's cursing out everybody, he's cursing the place and the nurses, the doctors. He's asking me if I still have my Bible and he's laughing real loud now, he's laughing so loud the other men are telling him to shut up, to be quiet and let them go to sleep. It's a madhouse, it's a crazy house, it's a wild zoo, and we're the animals, we're the animals all neatly tucked into these beds, waking up every morning puking at the green walls and smelling the urine on the floor. We're hurting and we're praying that we can get out of this place. Somebody, give us back our bodies!

And each day I train in an exercise room that is very crowded with broken men, bodies being bent and twisted, put up on the parallel bars. Our therapists, Jimmy and Dick, train us hard. We put on braces and crawl on the floor. We're pissing in our pants and crawling into the bathtub. We're jumping up and down the curb, learning how to use our wheelchairs. There is a big wheel in the corner and they're strapping a puny guy with glasses to it. I'm watching the clock and the kid is trying to spin the big wheel around. There are machines like the wheel all over the place, and there's pain on all the faces. Some of us are trying to laugh, we're talking about the beer that comes into the hospital in the brown paper bags. But you cannot mistake the pain. The kid with the long hair is in the hallway again, the kid who looks in and never does anything but look in.

Now I'm grabbing the weights, twenty-five-pound weights, I'm grabbing them and lifting them up and down, up and down, until my shoulders ache, until I can't lift anymore. I'm still lifting them even after that, I'm still lifting them and Jimmy is talking about his model airplanes and then he and Dick are lifting me up to the high bar. There are newly invented machines sold to the hospital by the government to make the men well, to take all the Willeys and the Garcias and make them well again, to fix these broken bodies. There are machines that make you stand again and machines that fix your hands again, but the only thing is that when it's all over, when the guys are pulled down from the machines, unstrapped from them, it's the same body, the same shattered broken man that went up on the rack moments before, and this is what we are all beginning to live with, this is what the kid standing in the hallway is saying with his eyes.

It's early in the afternoon. I'm standing on my braces, holding on to the parallel bars. My mother and little sister have just come through the doorway. It is the first chance for them to see me try to stand again. My mother is frightened, you can tell by the look on her face, and my sister is standing next to her trying to smile. They are holding each other's hands.

My legs are shaking in terrible spasms. They're putting thick straps around my waist and around my legs and now my arms start to shake furiously. My mother and sister are still standing in the hallway. They haven't decided to come into the room yet. Jimmy is strapping my arms along the pole and my big oversized blue hospital pants are falling down below my waist. My rear end is sticking out and Jimmy is smiling, looking over to my mother in the corner.

"See," says Jimmy, "he's standing."

I start throwing up all over the place, all over the blue hospital shirt and onto the floor, just below the machine. Jimmy quickly undoes the straps and puts me back in the chair. My sister and my mother are clutching each other, holding real tight to each other's hands.

"It's really a great machine," Jimmy says. "We have a couple more coming in real soon."

I turn the chair toward the window and look out across the Harlem River to where the cars are going over the bridge like ants.

3

FOR ME IT began in 1946 when I was born on the Fourth of July. The whole sky lit up in a tremendous fireworks display and my mother told me the doctor said I was a real firecracker. Every birthday after that was something the whole country celebrated. It was a proud day to be born on.

I hit a home run my first time at bat in the Massapequa Little League, and I can still remember my Mom and Dad and all the rest of the kids going crazy as I rounded the bases on seven errors and slid into home a hero. We lost the game to the Midgets that night, 22 to 7, and I cried all the way home. It was a long time ago, but sometimes I can still hear them shouting out in front of Pete's house on Hamilton Avenue. There was Bobby Zimmer, the tall kid from down the street, Kenny and Pete, little Tommy Law, and my best friend Richie Castiglia, who lived across from us on Lee Place.

Baseball was good to me and I played it all I

could. I got this baseball mitt when I was seven. I had to save up my allowance for it and cash in some soda bottles. It was a cheap piece of shit, but it seemed pretty nice, I mean it seemed beautiful to me before Bobby and some of the other guys tore the hell out of it.

I remember that I loved baseball more than anything else in the world and my favorite team was the New York Yankees. Every chance I got I watched the games on the TV in my house with Castiglia, waiting for Mickey Mantle to come to the plate. We'd turn up the sound of the television as the crowd went wild roaring like thunder. I'd run over to Richie's house screaming to his mother to tell Richie that Mantle was at bat.

And Richie would come running over with his mitt making believe we were at Yankee Stadium sitting in our box seats right in back of the Yankee dugout and when Mantle hit a homer you could hear the TV halfway down the block. Richie and I would go completely nuts hugging each other and jumping up and down with tears streaming down our faces. Mantle was our hero. He was like a god to us, a huge golden statue standing in center field. Every time the cameras showed him on the screen I couldn't take my eyes off him.

Back then the Yankees kept winning like they would never stop. It was hard to remember them ever losing, and when we weren't watching them on TV or down at the stadium, Kenny Goodman and I were at Parkside Field playing catch-a-fly-you're-up for hours with a beat-up old baseball we kept together with black electrician's tape. We played all day long out there, running across that big open field with all our might, diving and sliding face-first into the grass, making one-handed, spectacular catches. I used to make believe I was Mel Allen, screaming at the top of my lungs, "Did you see that?! Did you see that, folks?! Kovic has just made a tremendous catch and the crowd is going wild! They're jumping up and down all over the stadium! What a catch, ladies and gentlemen, what a tremendous catch by Kovic!" And I did that all afternoon, running back and forth across the gigantic field. I was Mickey Mantle, Willie Mays, and all my heroes, rolled into one.

When we weren't down at the field or watching the Yankees on TV, we were playing whiffle ball and climbing trees checking out birds' nests, going down to Fly Beach in Mrs. Zimmer's old car that honked the horn every time it turned the corner, diving underwater with our masks, kicking with our rubber frog's feet, then running in and out of our sprinklers when we got home, waiting for our turn in the shower. And during the summer nights we were all over the neighborhood, from Bobby's house to Kenny's, throwing gliders, doing handstands and backflips off fences, riding to the woods at the end of the block on our bikes, making rafts, building tree forts, jumping across the streams with tree branches, walking and balancing along the back fence like Houdini, hopping along the slate path all around the back yard seeing how far we could go on one foot.

And I ran wherever I went. Down to the school, to the candy store, to the deli, buying baseball cards and Bazooka bubblegum that had the little fortunes at the bottom of the cartoons.

When the Fourth of July came, there were fireworks going off all over the neighborhood. It was the most exciting time of year for me next to Christmas. Being born on the exact same day as my country I thought was really great. I was so proud. And every Fourth of July, I had a birthday party and all my friends would come over with birthday presents and we'd put on silly hats and blow these horns my Dad brought home from the A&P. We'd eat lots of ice cream and watermelon and I'd open up all the presents and blow out the candles on the big red, white, and blue birthday cake and then we'd all sing "Happy Birthday" and "I'm a Yankee Doodle Dandy." At night everyone would pile into Bobby's mother's old car and we'd go down to the drive-in, where we'd watch the fireworks display. Before the movie started, we'd all get out and sit up on the roof of the car with our blankets wrapped around us watching the rockets and Roman candles going up and exploding into fountains of rainbow colors, and later after Mrs. Zimmer dropped me off, I'd lie on my bed feeling a little sad that it all had to end so soon. As I closed my eyes I could still hear strings of firecrackers and cherry bombs going off all over the neighborhood.

The whole block grew up watching television. There was Howdy Doody and Rootie Kazootie, Cisco Kid and Gabby Hayes, Roy Rogers and Dale Evans. The Lone Ranger was on Channel 7. We watched cartoons for hours on Saturdays—Beanie and Cecil, Crusader Rabbit, Woody Woodpecker— and a show with puppets called Kukla, Fran, and Ollie. I sat on the rug in the living room watching Captain Video take off in his spaceship and saw thousands of savages killed by Ramar of the Jungle.

I remember Elvis Presley on the Ed Sullivan Show and my sister Sue going crazy in the living room jumping up and down. He kept twanging this big guitar and wiggling his hips, but for some reason they were mostly showing just the top of him. My mother was sitting on the couch with her hands folded in her lap like she was praying, and my dad was in the other room talking about how the Church had advised us all that Sunday that watching Elvis Presley could lead to sin.

I loved God more than anything else in the world back then and I prayed to Him and the Virgin Mary and Jesus and all the saints to be a good boy and a good American. Every night before I went to sleep I knelt down in front of my bed, making the sign of the cross and cupping my hands over my face, sometimes praying so hard I would cry. I asked every night to be good enough to make the major leagues someday. With God anything was possible. I made my first Holy Communion with a cowboy hat on my head and two six-shooters in my hands.

On Saturday nights, Mrs. Jacket drove us to confession, where we waited in line to tell the priest our sins, then walked out of the church feeling refreshed and happy with God and the world again. And then Dad and I and the rest of the kids went to church on Sundays. The church was a big place. It was the most enormous place I'd ever seen, with real quiet people sitting up straight and mumbling things. And I remember smelling this stuff and seeing the priest moving back and forth behind the altar, speaking in words we never understood.

And the Sunday comics and Dad cooking big breakfasts of hash brown potatoes and eggs, filling our bellies and making us feel warm and good inside. After breakfast I read the colorful comics on the living-room rug. There was Dick Tracy and Beetle Bailey, Dagwood and Blondie, Terry and the Pirates, Prince Valiant and Donald Duck, Dondi and Mickey Mouse, Bugs Bunny, Uncle Scrooge and Gasoline Alley.

My father was a checker at the A&P. He worked real hard. He was like a big hurricane, always moving with his big strong arms, raking the leaves in the back yard or building new parts to our little house. One summer I remember hammering nails on the roof with him and feeling proud to be up there with him doing all that hard work. Sometimes, he'd get angry because all of us weren't working, or cleaning or just acting busy. It seemed important to be moving whenever he was around and acting busy if you didn't have anything to do.

We were always moving, all the kids on the block and me, like there was no tomorrow. We cut up our mothers' broomsticks, hiding the brooms in the basement and taking the sticks out to

Hamilton Avenue for that night's stickball game, where we'd belt high-bouncing Spalding balls for hours off Kenny's roof and into little Tommy Law's hedge. We hit eggballs that used to spin crazily sideways with everyone screaming "Eggball! Eggball!" seeing if the guy who was pitching on one bounce could handle the lopsided pop-up. Whoever hit the ball past the second telephone pole right in back of Kenny's father's station wagon, or over Tommy Law's hedge, made a home run. We played every night in the spring and the summer until it was dark and the only light left on Hamilton Avenue was the street lamp.

We collected Topps baseball cards of our favorite players and traded them and flipped them and scaled them down against the wall at Turner's Bar.

In the spring we dug up worms and went fishing with Bobby Zimmer. I made a Morse code set with Castiglia, stringing the telegraph wires across the street to his house. We did science experiments with his chemistry set and Bobby and I played red-light-green-light on summer nights when Mom was taking the clothes off the line. And when it got dark my sister Sue and I chased fireflies with glass jars.

In the fall we played touch football in the streets and raked the summer leaves that had turned brown and fallen from the trees. We and our fathers swept them and piled them and packed them into wire baskets by the sides of our houses, burning them and watching the bright embers swirl in the wind. And the trees again stood naked in the back yard like they did every fall and winter and the air became fresh and cold and soon there was ice on the puddles in the streets outside our houses.

We'd all go back to school and for me it was always a frightening experience. I could never understand what was happening there. I remember once they called my mother and told her I had been staring out the window. I tried to listen to them, and sit in the chair behind the desk like they told me to, but I kept looking out that window at the trees and the sky. I couldn't wait until the last day of school when we all ran out of our classrooms, jumping up and down, throwing our books in the air, singing and shouting "No more pencils, no more books, no more teachers' dirty looks!" We were free. And another summer vacation began for all of us on the block.

When the first snow came we'd get our sleds out of the basement and belly-whop on sheets of ice out on Lee Place in front of Richie's house. We had snowball fights and built snow forts and snowmen. Castiglia and I and Bobby Zimmer used to grab the back bumpers of cars and see how far we could slide down the street on our shoes. Kenny and I would hide in Parkside Woods plastering the cars that passed along the boulevard with ice balls, then get Bobby and Pete and the rest of the guys and go down to Suicide Hill, a tremendous steep hill by the woods, frozen like glass, with a tree stump at the bottom you had to swerve around. Me and Bobby would head straight for it, and just before we were about to hit it,

I'd jam the wooden steering bar with my foot, throwing up sparks and ice, just missing the stump by inches. Then both of us would spin off the sled, rolling down the hill on top of each other, around and around, laughing into a huge snowdrift. We made winter gloves out of our father's socks, packing snowballs with them until they became soaked and frozen and our fingers would become numb and we'd have to take them off. I loved when it snowed, and so did all the rest of the guys on the block.

Every Saturday afternoon we'd all go down to the movies in the shopping center and watch gigantic prehistoric birds breathe fire, and war movies with John Wayne and Audie Murphy. Bobbie's mother always packed us a bagful of candy. I'll never forget Audie Murphy in *To Hell and Back*. At the end he jumps on top of a flaming tank that's just about to explode and grabs the machine gun blasting it into the German lines. He was so brave I had chills running up and down my back, wishing it were me up there. There were gasoline flames roaring around his legs, but he just kept firing that machine gun. It was the greatest movie I ever saw in my life.

Castiglia and I saw *The Sands of Iwo Jima* together. The Marine Corps hymn was playing in the background as we sat glued to our seats, humming the hymn together and watching Sergeant Stryker, played by John Wayne, charge up the hill and get killed just before he reached the top. And then they showed the men raising the flag on Iwo Jima with the marines' hymn still playing, and Castiglia and I cried in our seats. I loved the song so much, and every time I heard it I would think of John Wayne and the brave men who raised the flag on Iwo Jima that day. I would think of them and cry. Like Mickey Mantle and the fabulous New York Yankees, John Wayne in *The Sands of Iwo Jima* became one of my heroes.

We'd go home and make up movies like the ones we'd just seen or the ones that were on TV night after night. We'd use our Christmas toys—the Matty Mattel machine guns and grenades, the little green plastic soldiers with guns and flamethrowers in their hands. My favorites were the green plastic men with bazookas. They blasted holes through the enemy. They wiped them out at thirty feet just above the coffee table. They dug in on the front lawn and survived countless artillery attacks. They burned with high-propane lighter fluid and a quarter-gallon of gasoline or were thrown into the raging fires of autumn leaves blasting into a million pieces.

On Saturdays after the movies all the guys would go down to Sally's Woods—Pete and Kenny and Bobbie and me, with plastic battery-operated machine guns, cap pistols, and sticks. We turned the woods into a battlefield. We set ambushes, then led gallant attacks, storming over the top, bayonetting and shooting anyone who got in our way. Then we'd walk out of the woods like the heroes we knew we would become when we were men.

The army had a show on Channel 2 called "The

Big Picture," and after it was over Castiglia and I crawled all over the back yard playing guns and army, making commando raids all summer into Ackerman's housing project blasting away at the imaginary enemy we had created right before our eyes, throwing dirt bombs and rocks into the windows, making loud explosions like hand grenades with our voices then charging in with our Matty Mattel machine guns blazing. I bandaged up the German who was still alive and had Castiglia question him as I threw a couple more grenades, killing even more Germans. We went on countless missions and patrols together around my back yard, attacking Ackerman's housing project with everything from bazookas to flamethrowers and baseball bats. We studied the Marine Corps Guidebook and Richie brought over some beautiful pamphlets with very sharp-looking marines on the covers. We read them in my basement for hours and just as we dreamed of playing for the Yankees someday, we dreamed of becoming United States Marines and fighting our first war and we made a solemn promise that year that the day we turned seventeen we were both going down to the marine recruiter at the shopping center in Levittown and sign up for the United States Marine Corps.

We joined the cub scouts and marched in parades on Memorial Day. We made contingency plans for the cold war and built fallout shelters out of milk cartons. We wore spacesuits and space helmets. We made rocket ships out of cardboard boxes. And one Saturday afternoon in the base-

ment Castiglia and I went to Mars on the couch
we had turned into a rocket ship. We read books
about the moon and Wernher von Braun. And the
whole block watched a thing called the space race
begin. On a cold October night Dad and I watched
the first satellite, called *Sputnik*, moving across
the sky above our house like a tiny bright star. I
still remember standing out there with Dad looking up in amazement at that thing moving in the
sky above Massapequa. It was hard to believe that
this thing, this *Sputnik*, was so high up and moving so fast around the world, again and again.
Dad put his hand on my shoulder that night and
without saying anything I quietly walked back
inside and went to my room thinking that the
Russians had beaten America into space and
wondering why we couldn't even get a rocket off
the pad.

It seemed that whole school year we talked
about nothing but rockets and how they would
break away into stages and blast their satellites
into outer space. I got all the books I could on
rockets and outer space and read them for hours
in the library, completely fascinated by the draw-
ings and the telescopes and the sky charts. I had
an incredible rocket I got for Christmas that you
had to pump compressed water into. I pulled back
a plastic clip and it would send the thing blasting
out across Castiglia's lawn, then out onto Hamilton Avenue in a long arc of spurting water. Castiglia and I used to tape aluminum-foil rolls from
Mom's kitchen to the top of the plastic rocket then
put ants and worms in the nosecone with a secret

message wrapped in tissue paper. We had hundreds of rocket launchings that year. Though none of our payloads made it into orbit like the Sputniks, we had a lot of fun trying.

In the spring of that year I remember the whole class went down to New York City and saw the movie *Around the World in Eighty Days* on a tremendous screen that made all of us feel like we were right there in the balloon flying around the world. After the movie we went to the Museum of Natural History, where Castiglia and I walked around staring up at the huge prehistoric dinosaurs billions of years old, and studied fossils inside the big glass cases and wondered what it would have been like if we had been alive back then. After the museum they took us to the Hayden Planetarium, where the whole sixth-grade class leaned back in special sky chairs, looking up into the dome where a projector that looked like a huge mechanical praying mantis kept us glued to the sky above our heads with meteor showers and comets and galaxies that appeared like tremendous snowstorms swirling in the pitch darkness of the incredible dome. They showed the whole beginning of the earth that afternoon, as we sat back in our chairs and dreamed of walking on the moon someday or going off to Mars wondering if there really was life there and rocketing off deeper and deeper into space through all the time barriers into places and dreams we could only begin to imagine. When we got on the school bus afterward and were all seated, Mr. Serby, our sixth-grade teacher, turned around and in a soft voice told us that someday men would walk upon the moon, and probably in our lifetime, he said, we would see it happen.

We were still trying to catch up with the Russians when I heard on the radio that the United States was going to try and launch its first satellite, called *Vanguard*, into outer space. That night Mom and Dad and me and the rest of the kids watched the long pencil-like rocket on the television screen as it began to lift off after the countdown. It lifted off slowly at first. And then, almost as if in slow motion, it exploded into a tremendous fireball on the launching pad. It had barely gotten off the ground, and I cried that night in my living room. I cried watching *Vanguard* that night on the evening news with Mom and all the rest. It was a sad day for our country, I thought, it was a sad day for America. We had failed in our first attempt to put a satellite into orbit. I walked slowly back to my room. We were losing, I thought, we were losing the space race, and America wasn't first anymore.

When *Vanguard* finally made it into space, I was in junior high school, and right in the middle of the class the loudspeaker interrupted us and the principal in a very serious voice told us that something very important was about to happen. He talked about history, and how important the day was, how America was finally going to launch its first satellite and we would remember it for a long time.

There was a long countdown as we all sat on the edge of our seats, tuning our ears in to the radio. And then the rocket began to lift off the edge of the launching pad. In the background there was the tremendous roar of the rocket engines and a guy was screaming like Mel Allen that the rocket was lifting off. "It's lifting off! It's lifting off!" he kept screaming crazily. All the kids were silent for a few seconds, still straining in their chairs, waiting to see whether the rocket would make it or not, then the whole room broke into cheers and applause. America had done it! We had put our first satellite into space. "We did it! We did it!" the guy was screaming at the top of his lungs.

And now America was finally beginning to catch up with the Russians and each morning before I went to school I was watching "I Led Three Lives" on television about this guy who joins the Communists but is actually working for us. And I remember thinking how brave he was, putting his life on the line for his country, making believe he was a Communist, and all the time being on our side, getting information from them so we could keep the Russians from taking over our government. He seemed like a very serious man, and he had a wife and a kid and he went to secret meetings, calling his friends comrades in a low voice, and talking through newspapers on park benches.

The Communists were all over the place back then. And if they weren't trying to beat us into outer space, Castiglia and I were certain they were infiltrating our schools, trying to take over our classes and control our minds. We were both certain that one of our teachers was a secret Communist agent and in our next secret club meeting we promised to report anything new he said during our next history class. We watched him very carefully that year. One afternoon he told us that China was going to have a billion people someday. "One billion!" he said, tightly clenching his fist. "Do you know what that means?" he said, staring out the classroom window. "Do you know what that's going to mean?" he said in almost a whisper. He never finished what he was saying and after that Castiglia and I were convinced he was definitely a Communist.

About that time I started doing push-ups in my room and squeezing rubber balls until my arms began to ache, trying to make my body stronger and stronger. I was fascinated by the muscle-men ads in the beginnings of the Superman comics, showing how a skinny guy could overnight transform his body into a hulk of fighting steel, and each day I increased the push-ups, more and more determined to build a strong and healthy body. I made muscles in the mirror for hours and checked my biceps each day with a tape measure, and did pull-ups on a bar in the doorway of my room before I went to school each morning. I was a little guy, back then, and used to put notches with a penny on the door of my room, little scratches with the coin to remind myself how tall I was and to see each week whether I'd grown.

"The human body is an amazing thing," the coaches told us that fall when we started high school. "It is a beautiful remarkable machine that will last you a lifetime if you care for it properly." And we listened to them, and worked and trained our young bodies until they were strong and quick.

I joined the high-school wrestling team, practicing and working out every day down in the basement of Massapequa High School. The coaches made us do sit-ups, push-ups, and spinning drills until sweat poured from our faces and we were sure we'd pass out. "Wanting to win and wanting to be first, that's what's important," the coaches told us. "Play fair, but play to win," they said. They worked us harder and harder until we thought we couldn't take it anymore and then they would yell and shout for us to keep going and drive past all the physical pain and discomfort. "More! More!" they screamed. "If you want to win, then you're going to have to work! You're going to have to drive your bodies far beyond what you think you can do. You've got to pay the price for victory! You can always go further than you think you can."

Wrestling practice ended every day with wind sprints in the basement hallways that left us gasping for air and running into the showers bent over in pain, and I honestly wondered sometimes what I was doing there in the first place and why I was allowing myself to go through all this.

The wrestling coach was very dedicated and held practice every day of the week including Saturdays and Sundays and I can even remember having practice once on Thanksgiving. I came in

first in the Christmas wrestling tournament.
There's still a picture of me in one of the old
albums in the attic that shows me with two other
guys holding a cardboard sign with the word
Champion on it. I won most of my matches that
year. When I lost, I cried just like when I lost my
Little League games and I'd jump on the bus and
ride back to Massapequa with tears in my eyes,
not talking to anyone for hours sometimes.

I was very shy back then and dreamed of having a girlfriend, or just someone to hold my hand.
Even though I was on the wrestling team and had
won all those matches and wore my sweater with
the big *M* on it, I still dreamed of the day I could
have a girlfriend like all the rest of the guys. I
wanted to be hoisted aloft in the arms of other
young men like myself and carried off the field for
scoring the winning touchdown, or winning the
wrestling match that brought the championship
to my school.

I wanted to be a hero.

I wanted to be stared at and talked about in the
hallways.

"Hey look," said one of the kids. "There goes
Kovic!"

I was the great silent athlete now, who never
had to say anything, who walked through the
halls of Massapequa High School, sucking the air
deeply into my chest and pumping up the blood
into my arms.

"There goes Kovic," a pretty freshman said.
"Boy, he sure is cute." And as I walked through
the crowded halls I was sure everyone was notic-

ing me, staring at my varsity letter, and looking
at my wrestler's shoulders.

And it was also during my freshman year that
I started to get pimples on my face. I remember
coming home from school and seeing what looked
like a tremendous blackhead on my forehead. It
was right smack-dab in the middle of my forehead
and it was just like the things that were all over
my sister Sue's face. The more I looked in the
mirror, the more scared I got. Stevie Jacket's face
was covered with the things, he had the worst
case of them of anyone I ever knew in my life.
In gym I saw him once taking a shower, and his
face and neck, all over his arms and back, his
whole body was covered with blackheads and
whiteheads and thousands of pimples. And now I
was catching them, I was getting them just like
Stevie Jacket and my sister. There it was, right
in front of me in the mirror, a big goddamn blackhead, and after staring at it for almost an hour,
I still didn't know what to do. I remembered this
girl in the sixth grade who used to have them all
over her face and it looked like somebody hit her
with a rake. It was awful and she used to put this
disgusting filmy cream on, to try and hide them,
but it looked worse.

I looked in the medicine cabinet for the little
metal thing that my sister used, with tiny open-
ings on each end that you were supposed to press
against the pimples and pop them out of your
skin forever. So I pressed it up against the blackhead real hard like I was going to take my head
off, until it finally oozed out of the pore like a tiny

white dot. I kept popping those things all year, and I finally broke down and bought that filmy crap, and started to put it on my face too.

It was about the same time I started to get these ugly hairs under my lip and up in my armpits. I was getting these things all happening at once, and I couldn't stop them, no matter how hard I tried, they all kept coming. I put some Nair under my lip one night because one of the guys in boy scout camp had said that if you shaved with a razor it would grow back twice as fast. So I put on this underarm stuff I found in the closet, it was the stuff that was supposed to take the hair off your legs. Well, I put it under my nose and waited about an hour and then I wiped it off, leaving a big red rash. It looked like a huge gigantic red mustache and I went to school the next week using a handkerchief, trying to hide it and making believe I had a real bad cold. Most of the year was like that, with the pimples all over my face, and by the time the spring came all sorts of other difficult things began to happen.

I felt strange feelings in places I had never discovered before. The part of me that had just been there like everything else now began to get hard and excited every time I looked at a pretty girl. I had never felt anything like it before in my life. That thing, my penis, was getting hard, every time I watched the girls on "American Bandstand" or saw them walking down the streets. They'd even be in my dreams at night. I'd wake up in the mornings with the whole sheet soaked. I felt guilty at first. I actually thought I was committing a sin, dreaming it, thinking it, just watching them. But then one afternoon I crawled on top of a Rawlings basketball in my bedroom and did it for the sheer pleasure of doing it. And it felt good. It felt so good that I did it again after that, and again, and again—with teddy bears in my bed making believe they were Marilyn Monroe, in the bathroom in the bathtub, in the basement laying the side pocket of the pool table seventeen times, in the back yard against trees. I did it everywhere. And no matter how hard I tried I couldn't stop. It got so bad after a while, I started saying Acts of Contrition after doing it. I asked God to forgive me for feeling this thing and then I couldn't understand why I'd be asking God to forgive me for doing something that felt so good.

For some reason Mom and I just didn't get along back then. I was being sent to my room for punishment almost every night after dinner. "Take a bath," "Clean your room," "Take out the garbage." . . . It was always something like that, and after battling it out with Mom in the kitchen and getting hit with the egg turner I'd be back in my room cursing her out under my breath as she'd be shouting, "God's going to punish you, Ronnie! God's going to punish you!" Later she'd come in and tell me she was sorry for yelling at me and I'd give her a big hug and tell her I was sorry too for making her so angry.

Mom always wanted me to be the best at whatever I did, especially at school. "If you fail any subjects this year," she'd tell me, "you're not going out for any sports." I kept telling her I was trying to do my best, but the only thing I could think of was baseball and instead of doing my homework every night I read every sports book I could get my hands on. For hours I'd swing the baseball bat in front of the mirror in my room. I still wanted to play for the New York Yankees more than anything else in the world.

I joined the track team in the spring. I wanted to be the greatest pole-vaulter in the history of the school and so I worked out every day until dark on the parallel bars Dad had built the summer before in the back yard. I remember Mom in the kitchen cheering me on, turning on the porch lights so I could work out even more. I loved those bars and when my brother Tommy was home from school, we'd both get on them together. We'd call Mom and Dad out to watch us perform, doing handstands together, back to back, with both of us touching each other's feet. "The amazing Kovics," I'd shout to Mom. "Ladies and gentlemen, the amazing Kovics are about to perform their death-defying feats." I can still remember both of them standing below us with pride in their eyes as we turned and balanced on those bars. I'd swing my body back and forth, back and forth, until I had swept myself into a perfect handstand, my body in a strong beautiful arc above my back yard. I'd look out around me, holding the handstand as long as I could, and swing down, dismounting with a beautiful twist, thumping onto the ground, stinging my bare feet. It was perfect, I'd say to myself, beautiful, just beautiful.

I was a natural athlete, and there wasn't much of anything I wasn't able to do with my body back then. I was proud and confident and there was always a tremendous energetic bounce in the way I moved. I knew what it was to walk and run and I loved it. After climbing the ropes in school, I'd go out to the track. I remember the feel of the long, lightweight, fiberglass pole in my hands and the black Permatrack beneath my feet; even in the meets I'd jump without shoes. I'd start running from the very end of the long track toward the pit, with the sleek pole gently vibrating up and down in my hands and my face full of determination. I'd hit the hole with the end of my pole, swinging like a pendulum, then kick high into the air, twisting, clearing the bar by inches, falling into the pit on my back, looking at the bar still up there.

As I got older Mom would kid me a lot because I wasn't interested in girls, but I was still dreaming about them all the time. I thought constantly about Joan Marfe, the girl who'd sat next to me in sixth grade, but I was too shy to ever ask her for a date.

I'd heard a priest at some kind of church conference warn us how a thing called petting could lead to sin. Kissing was all right, the priest said in a serious voice, but petting or heavy petting almost always led to sex, and sex, he said, was a mortal sin. I remember listening to him that day and promising myself and God I'd try never to get too close to a girl. I wanted to do all the things the guys in the study hall whispered about, but I didn't want to offend God. I never even went to the senior or junior prom. I just wanted to be a great athlete and a good Catholic and maybe even a priest someday or a major leaguer.

In the spring of the year before I graduated I actually wrote a letter to the New York Yankees management telling them I would give anything in the world for a tryout at the stadium. Castiglia's sister Arlene typed it up for me and for weeks I walked around in a daze waiting for an answer, daydreaming about how Dad and Castiglia would drop me off at the Long Island Railroad station that day and shake my hand and wish me luck. I'd be looking at them, pounding my fist into my new baseball mitt: "I'm gonna make it. Don't worry about it, Castig. I'm gonna make it." Then there'd be the great moment after the tryout when one of the coaches would come up to me: "Well, Kovic, you really looked good out there today. We think you've got what it takes."

It never happened that way. Even though the letter from the Yankees finally came in the mail and I ran over to Castiglia's house shouting that I had made the tryouts, I chickened out when the morning came to leave for the station. I decided I didn't want to go after all. Richie and Bobby Zimmer were all over me for weeks, and I was sorry I'd ever told them anything. I still played after that, but it was different. I was thinking about other things, other things I wanted to be.

By that fall it seemed the guys on the block were almost grown up. In the halls at school we still gave each other the old Woodchuck Club signal we had started in sixth grade, sticking our hands under our chins, moving our fingers up and down, shouting, "Woodchuck, woodchuck." It was crazy but it kept us together. And we went from class to class just waiting for each day to end so we could get back home and play touch out on the street after our homework. Still everything was different. Castiglia was still talking about being a priest or joining the marines, but we weren't seeing as much of each other anymore. Bobby Zimmer told me one afternoon that Richie was growing his hair long and smoking cigarettes with Peter Weber in some abandoned cement tunnel in the woods at the end of the block.

Bobby's hair was long too. My mother said he had a pompadour just like Elvis Presley's. Whenever I saw him in the hallways, he had a pretty girl by his side and he was the first one of the guys on the block to get a driver's license. I was still shy with girls. While I'd be waiting at the bus stop every morning with Kenny and Mike Lamb, Bobby Zimmer would drive past honking the horn of his car with one arm around his girlfriend. He'd turn the corner on Hamilton Avenue, roaring off down Broadway to the high school, leaving the rest of us still jumping up and down at the bus stop trying to stay warm. Peter Weber and Castiglia also drove to school every morning or got rides with their new friends.

I remember for a long time Mike and Bobby Zimmer were a lot taller than me and Castiglia. Then all of a sudden I was taller than all three of them. We'd stand back to back over at Kenny's house as his mother checked to see who was the tallest and it was so good for little guys like me and Castiglia to be taller than the other guys. And when we weren't trying to see who was the tallest, we'd be out on the lawn still playing tag and wrestling on the grass.

Steve Jacket was still throwing screwdrivers into his front lawn across from Pete's house on Hamilton Avenue, telling us all he was going to become a TV sports announcer just like Mel Allen, and Pete was still coming over to my house every once in a while after school to steal beer out of my father's locker in the garage. Little Tommy Law was hanging out with Billy Meyers, trying to stay out of trouble and graduate from high school like the rest of us.

High school was just about over for me and the rest of the guys. We had been on the block together for almost twelve years, running and moving from Toronto Avenue to Lee Place to Hamilton Avenue. No one could remember how we all first got together back then, but we had become friends, "as close as real brothers," Peter told me one afternoon, and we wanted to believe it would always be that way.

President Kennedy got killed that last year and we played football in the huge snowdrifts that had settled on the Long Island streets that afternoon. We played in silence, I guess because you're supposed to be silent when someone dies. I truly felt I had lost a dear friend. I was deeply hurt for a long time afterward. We went to the movies that

Sunday. I can't remember what was playing, but how ashamed I was that I was even there, that people could sit through a movie or have the nerve to want to go to football games when our president had been killed in Dallas. The pain stuck with me for a long time after he died. I still remember Oswald being shot and screaming to my mother to come into the living room. It all seemed wild and crazy like some Texas shootout, but it was real for all of us back then, it was very real. I remember Johnson being sworn in on the plane and the fear in the eyes of the woman judge from Texas. And then the funeral and the casket. I guess all of us, the whole country, watched it like a big football game. Down the street the black horses came and his little boy saluting the way he did, the perfect way he did. Soon after he died there was a memorial picture of him that went up in the candy store down the block. At the bottom of it it said he had been born in 1917 and had died in 1963. It stayed up in the candy store on the wall for a long time after we all went to the war.

That spring before I graduated, my father took me down to the shopping center in Levittown and made me get my first job. It was in a supermarket not far from the marine recruiting station. I worked stacking shelves and numbing my fingers and hands unloading cases of frozen food from the trucks. Working with Kenny each day after school, all I could think of, day after day, was joining the marines. My legs and my back ached, but I knew that soon I would be signing the papers and leaving home.

I didn't want to be like my Dad, coming home from the A&P every night. He was a strong man, a good man, but it made him so tired, it took all the energy out of him. I didn't want to be like that, working in that stinking A&P, six days a week, twelve hours a day. I wanted to be somebody. I wanted to make something out of my life.

I was getting older now, I was seventeen, and I looked at myself in the mirror that hung from the back of the door in my room and saw how tall and strong I had suddenly become. I took a deep breath, flexing my muscles, and stared straight into the mirror, turning to the side and looking at myself for a long time.

In the last month of school, the marine recruiters came and spoke to my senior class. They marched, both in perfect step, into the auditorium with their dress blue uniforms and their magnificently shined shoes. It was like all the movies and all the books and all the dreams of becoming a hero come true. I watched them and listened as they stood in front of all the young boys, looking almost like statues and not like real men at all. They spoke in loud voices and one of them was tall and the other was short and very strong looking.

"Good afternoon men," the tall marine said, "We have come today because they told us that some of you want to become marines." He told us that the marines took nothing but the best, that

if any of us did not think we were good enough,
we should not even think of joining. The tall marine spoke in a very beautiful way about the exciting history of the marines and how they had
never lost and America had never been defeated.

"The marines have been the first in everything,
first to fight and first to uphold the honor of our
country. We have served on distant shores and at
home, and we have always come when our country has called. There is nothing finer, nothing
prouder, than a United States Marine."

When they were finished, they efficiently picked
up their papers and marched together down the
steps of the stage to where a small crowd of boys
began to gather. I couldn't wait to run down after
them, meet with them and shake their hands. And
as I shook their hands and stared up into their
eyes, I couldn't help but feel I was shaking hands
with John Wayne and Audie Murphy. They told
us that day that the Marine Corps built men—
body, mind, and spirit. And that we could serve
our country like the young president had asked
us to do.

We were all going in different directions and
we had our whole lives ahead of us, and a million different dreams. I can still remember the
last stickball game. I stood at home plate with the
sun in my face and looked out at Richie, Pete, and
the rest. It was our last summer together and the
last stickball game we ever played on Hamilton
Avenue.

One day that summer I quit my job at the food

store and went to the little red, white, and blue shack in Levittown. My father and I went down together. It was September by the time all the paperwork was completed, September 1964. I was going to leave on a train one morning and become a marine.

I stayed up most of the night before I left, watching the late movie. Then "The Star-Spangled Banner" played. I remember standing up and feeling very patriotic, chills running up and down my spine. I put my hand over my heart and stood rigid at attention until the screen went blank.

"AWRIGHT, LADIES!" SHOUTED the sergeant again. "My name is Staff Sergeant Joseph. This—" he said, pointing to the short sergeant at the end of the formation, "this is Sergeant Mullins. I am your senior drill instructor. You will obey both of us. You will listen to everything we say. You will do everything we tell you to do. Your souls today may belong to God, but your asses belong to the United States Marine Corps!" The sergeant swaggered sharply back and forth in front of the formation, almost bouncing up and down on his heels, his long thin hands sliding up and down against his hips. "I want you swinging dicks to stand straight at attention, do you hear me? I don't want you people to look left or right, I want you people to stand straight ahead."

It was unbearably hot. He could feel the sweat rolling off his face. He was afraid to look either way and he stared straight ahead like he'd been told.

"Left face!" screamed the sergeant.

"You goddamned idiots!" screamed the short sergeant again. "You're turned the wrong way. You goddamned fucking people, you goddamned scum, when are you people gonna listen, when are you people gonna learn? You came here to be marines."

The short sergeant was laughing now. He took a deep breath and stepped forward, picking out one of the young boys, the tips of his shiny shoes almost touching the tips of the ones the boy wore. "You no good fucking civilian maggot," he screamed in the boy's ears. "You're worthless, do you understand? And I'm gonna kill you. There are eighty of you, eighty young warm bodies, eighty sweet little ladies, eighty sweetpeas, and I want you maggots to know today that you belong to me and you will belong to me until I have made you into marines."

The formation was very sloppy. It didn't look to him like a military formation at all. He was trying so hard, standing straight and looking ahead and cupping his hands right along the seams of his trousers the way the guidebook had taught him, the way Richie and he had practiced it so many times. He was straining till he felt his hands almost go numb, he was trying so hard to be a good marine and do what they said and boot camp hadn't even started yet. But he was determined, even though he didn't understand why they had to be so angry and so mean, why they had to scream and shout and curse the way they did. He couldn't understand that, but it didn't matter. He was going to make it, he was going to do what they said, like a good marine.

They took them from the place where they had stayed that night and marched them and ran them shouting and screaming, eighty of them, dressed in suits and ties and sweatshirts and T-shirts, long-haired and short-haired, short ones and fat ones, kids from New Jersey, kids from Detroit, the drill instructor almost stepping on the boys' heels, taunting and threatening, "Let's go! Let's go!" He looked up at the sky as he ran; he could hardly breathe.

"Awright, awright, all you maggots, get in there!"

They had come to what looked like a large hangar. And they marched, all eighty, single file, with their heads straight ahead, into the aluminum structure, with the chrome-domes they had just gotten spinning on their heads, their cartridge belts loosely fitted, jumping and dangling from their waists. They didn't look like marines, he thought, they looked like Richie and Pete and the rest of the guys, running into Sally's Woods for a game of guns. What was going on here? he thought. What was happening? It wasn't anything like he thought it would be. Why did they have to push them and shove them and kick them and scream and shout? But before he could even get his thoughts together, they put them in a long line and made them face a line of large wooden boxes. He saw that each box had a number painted on it.

"I want you to take your clothes off," the sergeant shouted. "I want you to take off everything that ever reminded you of being a civilian and put it in the box. Do you see that box in front of you and that number? I want everything!" he said. "Now do it, ladies! Quickly, now, quickly!"

As soon as the sergeant had said it, all the young boys began tearing their clothes off, unbuckling their belts, pulling off their shirts, their pants, their shoes, their socks. Everything went. Everything. And as they took their last bits of clothing off, the short sergeant began racing back and forth along the line, screaming into the ears of the young boys, cursing them and jabbing his hands hard into their backs.

He had a small medal around his neck. It was the one Mom had given him for Christmas. He had kept it on for years, all through high school, and even down in the basement wrestling practice, he had never taken it off. And now the short sergeant was pointing at it with his finger, laughing, then shouting for him to throw it in the box that had the number painted on the side.

"Can I keep it?" he said.

"Don't talk back to me," screamed the sergeant. "You fucking maggot. Don't you ever talk back to me!" The sergeant grabbed the medal from his hand and threw it in the box. And now he found himself turning slowly to where the thunderous sound of the drill instructor's voice came from, and he was moving now, stepping and marching, almost running, and then stepping again. He didn't know what to do. They were screaming in his ears again, shouting, cursing. The short guy punched him again and again, and he felt his breath burst from his lungs, twisting and bending him over.

"I'm trying," he said.

"Get in step!" screamed the sergeant.

Stepping, marching, running. "Get in step, people! Come on, people! Let's go, people!" He didn't know what to do. He didn't know how to do it. He wanted to go home, then he didn't. Then he wanted to, then he didn't know what he wanted to do. They were driving him and pushing him and shoving him, screaming and bullying him through this whole crazy thing. He kept thinking over and over and over again that this day, this place, the screaming shouting voices in his ears, in all their ears, roaring like thunder were like angry hate! Oh get us out! Get us out! God, help us!

And they threw them into a barbershop that was more like a factory where there was hair flying all over the place, his hair, everyone's hair, all the hair of the boys who had come to be marines that day. Men as angry and as cold as the sergeants shaved the hair off their heads until he could feel the warm soft wind that swept through the hangar on his head too. They had made them completely bald, and he looked around as he sat on the chair, and the guys who were cutting, the guys who were shaving all their hair off, weren't even looking at the heads, but just cutting like guys shearing sheep.

"Get the fuck up!" screamed the barber. "Next!" he shouted, and the next young boy jumped into the chair staring straight ahead.

He found himself being swept along with all the

young boys, now strange looking, naked like himself. Young bodies tense and twisted naked together, grasping on to each other, holding on like children. Where were they going? he thought. What were they becoming? Shoved and pushed by the drill instructors, they continued to move, from the barbershop where their heads had been shaved, through the long metal hallways of the hangar into the showers.

"Wash all that scum off!" screamed the sergeant. "I want you maggots to wash all that civilian scum off your bodies forever!" And now he felt the soothing hot water streaming down his back and onto his legs. Oh, he could feel it splash hot against his bald head. It felt so good, so warm and different from their angry screams. And before he could begin to even feel comfortable, someone was shouting at him again and telling him to get out of the shower, back into the place where he had been before, in front of his box again. And he ran with the others, their bodies naked and dripping with water, all eighty shaved and washed clean and their clothing packed tightly to be mailed home. And now they all stood rigid at attention, their hands at their sides, facing the boxes with the painted numbers.

"Awright people, awright people!" said the sergeant. "We're gonna issue you clothing." There were marine privates walking past the boxes throwing in green belts and trousers, utility caps and long black socks. "Awright ladies!" screamed the sergeant. "We are going to begin today by learning how to dress. I want you to look down

into your boxes and I want you to look for a pair
of black socks. Do you see that pair of black
socks, ladies?"

"Yessir!" screamed the eighty boys.

"Again!" shouted the sergeant.

"Yessir!" screamed the young men.

"Now I want you to grab that pair of black
socks, when I tell you to," he said, almost hesitating. "And when I tell you to grab them I want you
to put them on. Do you understand that, ladies?"

"Yessir!"

"Do it!" shouted the short sergeant. And one
hundred and sixty hands reached into the boxes,
searching for the black socks and putting them on
their feet as quickly as they could.

"Grab your trousers!" shouted the sergeant.
"These are trousers," he shouted. "Not pants!
Pants are for little girls! *Trousers* are for ma-
rines! Put your trousers on!" he commanded.

"Yessir!" they screamed and they grabbed their
trousers and then their belts and then their skivvy
shirts and jackets and utility caps, until they all
stood dressed together inside that hangar. Many
of the uniforms didn't fit. He could feel his cap
covering his face, he was almost swimming in it,
and his enormous pants hung down below his
boots that didn't fit either. He felt like a raga-
muffin doll. He thought he must look like some
kind of painter, with his painting cap turned all
sideways on his head. He felt so silly. He looked
around him and some of the others looked worse
than he did. There was one short kid who seemed

to have his belt buckle up to his chest and his hat seemed to cover his whole face too.

Why, there was a tall guy, to the right of him down at the end, yeah there was a tall guy whose pants were way too short and his shirt, he thought, belonged on the little kid who was swimming in his stuff. There was a fat kid who couldn't get his pants on at all and the drill instructor was screaming at him, cursing him, and telling him he'd never make it through boot camp alive, he'd never become a marine.

They were all crowding around the fat guy, all the drill instructors, there must have been six of them standing all around that fat kid, circling him for the kill with their angry stares and one at a time they'd scream into his ears, laughing at him and cursing him because he couldn't fit into his pants.

He kept looking from the corner of his eye, and all of them, all of them on the other side of the fat kid, they all seemed to be looking the way he was, trying to see what was going to happen next. And now he remembered that kid, he was the same one on the bus after they had landed in Raleigh, he was the same kid that had stood up and boasted on the bus, with both hands on his hips, that his father had won a whole lot of medals in World War II and he'd killed a whole bunch of Germans. Yeah, it was the same kid. The same one who told everyone he wasn't afraid of anything. Now they had him surrounded so you couldn't see what was happening, and they were punching him, yeah punching, he could hear that

fat kid shout every time they jabbed their tight
fists into his gut. And now he sounded like a little
whining three-year-old, he sounded like a little
baby, he was just like a little frightened baby.

"Are you gonna cry?" screamed the sergeant.
"Is that what's gonna happen? Everybody, I want
you to look at this, look over here, people, I want
you to see the baby cry!"

Everyone looked over to where the fat kid was.

"Are those tears?" screamed the sergeant. They
were all laughing now, laughing, rocking back
and forth on their heels, their hands on their hips.

"Cry!" screamed the sergeant. "Cry Cry Cry you
little baby! That's what we want, we want you
people to cry like little babies because that's all
you maggots are. You are nothing!"

The fat kid was now kneeling on the floor. His
whole body was shaking; he had his hands against
his face like he was praying. "I don't want this,"
he was saying. "I . . . I want . . . to go home. I
want to go home." He was saying it over and over
again now, "I want to go home, I want to go
home, I want to go home." He hadn't even gotten
there, it was the first day and he wanted to go
home. And as he watched, the drill instructors,
having had all the fun they could, slowly stepped
back from where the fat boy was kneeling, laughing and scorning him, pitying him and cursing
him, running back and forth screaming in the ears
of the other young boys, cursing them and jabbing them again and again, until the whole maddening thunderous echo of cursing sounds and
raging angry voices began to deafen his ears and

turn his head around and around till he wondered who he was and what was happening and what was this place.

"He's not gonna make it, he's not gonna make it!" screamed the short sergeant, almost dancing in front of them. "He's not gonna hack it. He's a baby. He's nothing but a baby, ladies!"

"He can't even fit into his pants!" screamed the tall sergeant, laughing.

"Yeah," said the southern sergeant. "He's nothin' but a goddamned little baby and you know what we do with babies," he said. "We kick 'em in their fucking asses and send 'em home. You people, you better listen up!" said the southern sergeant. "You are in Parris Island. You are now in Platoon One Hundred Eighty-one. You are in my platoon and if you people wanna be marines, y'all gonna hafta work harder than you have ever worked before in your lives and you are gonna listen to me and you are gonna do everything I tell you to do if you want to get your asses off this island alive and become marines you better listen to me."

It was beginning to get dark on the island. It had been a long day for him. It had seemed like a hundred days, a thousand days! The day had been endless. It was the longest day of his life. But, he thought, if this is what it takes to become a marine, he was ready to take it, and if this is what he would have to go through in the days and weeks ahead, then he was ready for it. Ready for it!

Like the young president had said, they would have to bear many burdens, many sacrifices, and now he was in this place, and as crazy and depressing as it seemed, he would face it like a man. He would not let his president, or his family, or any of them down. He could take it, he was tough, he knew it. He could make it through these thirteen weeks.

And now they shouted for them to move out of the hangar that they seemed to have been in forever.

"Right—face!" screamed the short sergeant. "Double time . . . MARCH!" screamed the sergeant again. And they began to move now, all eighty of them, with their fresh new clothing and their utility caps, their oversized belts hanging from their waists. They ran, dragging heavy sea bags packed full of new clothing and uniforms, like men bent in a gale. They stumbled and gasped across the huge parade deck past the great statue of the marines raising the flag at Iwo Jima, and he thought of John Wayne and the movies and Castiglia and for a moment his heart quickened. He felt good inside. He was proud of being on the island and getting the chance to become a marine.

They looked like little schoolchildren being herded toward the long wooden barracks, all eighty of them now, stretched out in a long line, tripping over their pants, their caps spinning crazily around their heads, gasping for air, choking and spitting and coughing in the heat, their oversized boots thumping against the parade deck again and again, thumping until they sounded like a train slowly rolling into the station. He felt he couldn't go on any farther and the drill instructors were still screaming. They had been screaming all day, all afternoon, all morning, ever since he got to that place they were screaming, screaming and shouting, cursing, screaming again, until it all sounded like one tremendous scream. He had to keep pushing, he thought. He had to make it to the long wooden squad bay. He had come this far, he thought. He hadn't cried like the fat boy, he hadn't fallen to his knees like a baby. He had come this far and he was gonna make it the rest of the way, with all of them.

But now some were dropping out in back of him. He could hear the drill instructors shouting at them. They were falling to their knees in the evening heat onto the parade deck and he looked back and watched, still gasping for air, still not believing he had made it this far. There were boys on their knees—three, four, five, six—he couldn't count them all, but they were on their knees with their sea bags still over their shoulders like Christs, and they were crawling, he saw them crawling! trying not to quit, trying to catch up with the rest. And he was thankful now he was still on his feet. Oh his legs ached and his chest felt like it was going to explode and his head was pounding now and his eyes were burning and he was getting closer and closer.

Some men were cursing now, swearing and cursing like the drill instructors, cursing the heat, cursing the sweat. They began to shout and curse the shock, the shock of this day. They dragged themselves, exhausted, in a single file into the squad bay. It was a long hallway painted green

with double racks on each side making the place
seem tighter than it was. He found a rack at the
end near the window that looked out into the
swamps. He stood rigid at attention in front of
his rack, dropping his sea bag at his side, staring
straight ahead like they had told him, staring
directly into the eyes of another young man. All of
them now were coming in, their big boots banging against the wooden deck, cursing and sweat-
ing and dragging their sea bags up to their racks.

"Get in there! Hurry up! Hurry up! Get in
there!" screamed the sergeant who came running
through the open door of the squad bay. "I want
each one of you to get in front of a rack!"
screamed the sergeant. "And now I want you to
listen to me!" And he told them that this place,
this squad bay, would be their home for the next
three months. They would live here and sleep
here and shower here and work here until they
became marines.

"It's late!" screamed the short sergeant. "And I
know how tired you ladies are tonight. Are you
tired ladies?" screamed the sergeant.

"Yessir!" shouted the men.

"I can't hear you!" screamed the sergeant.
"Louder!"

"Yessir!" the young men screamed again.

"That's more like it."

The sergeant repeated a long list of names including the president and vice president of the
United States and everyone else right on down
to the senior drill instructor himself, and after
completing the list, he shouted to the men that

every night from here on out they would repeat those names. And then he shouted, "Ready— Mount!" And they shouted back "Ready—Mount! Aye aye, sir!" And all eighty jumped into bed, still standing at attention, lying in their racks.

"Awright! I want you to stand at attention all night! I think it's good practice for you."

And as they lay in their racks at attention, one of the sergeants had a young black boy from Georgia sing the Lord's Prayer: "Our Father, Who art in heaven, hallo-o-wed be Thy name," he sang. "Thy kingdom come, Thy will be done, on earth as it is in hea-ven." And when he was finished the lights went out and they slowly closed their eyes.

And the first day had ended.

(*Lights flash, flash, flash standing by my rack now*) sir! the private requests to make an emergency sitting head call *WHAT DO YOU WANT KOVIC?* sir! o god o jesus yessir aye aye sir one two aye aye sir If I die in a combat zone pack me up and ship me home *COUNTDOWN—READY —SEATS! GET IN THE PASSAGEWAY SWEET-PEA AND GIVE ME FIVE HUNDRED BENDS AND THRUSTS—DO IT! BY THE LEFT FLANK* —one two three four I love the Marine Corps *THIS IS YOUR RIFLE LADIES I WANT YOU TO KNOW IT ALL OF IT EVERY PART OF IT! CAN'T YOU READ SWEETPEA?* this is my rifle this is my gun this is for fighting this is for fun, Ask not what your country (*the formation now*) remember *i can talk no i can't talk no i can't bring back by the river—with the rifle*—America. America. God shed His grace on thee, Eenie meenie mynie moe catch a nigger by the toe *EYES RIGHT! I WANT YOU TO BELIEVE THIS AFTERNOON THAT THIS THING OUT THERE IS A COMMIE SONOF-ABITCH* and wops and spics and chinks and japs and *GET IN FRONT OF YOUR RACKS!! THAT'S NOT QUICK ENOUGH!* (*never quick enough, eighteen i'm eighteen now*) *UP! DOWN! GET IT! OUT! GET IT! o mom o please o someone somone help now somebody BY THE RIGHT FLANK! GET DOWN! GET UP!* (*hot deck parades faces mirror face still pimples now boots and socks*) *o lights flashes GET THE FUCK UP!* We will bear any burden *by your leave sir excuse me sir pardon me sir* suffer any hardships *i'm sorry sir o yessir no sir aye aye sir, sir!* (*push-ups push-ups clanking sounds steel*) *READY—SEATS!* (*plates forks and*) *EAT AND HURRY UP AND RUN AND HURRY UP AND EAT AND HURRY UP AND RUN AND HURRY UP HURRY UP!* There is something I believe—we'll be home by Christmas Eve *sir my service number is two-oh-three-oh-two-six-one sir the president of the united states is the honorable lyndon baines johnson sir the vice president is* Our Father, Who art in heaven *PREPARE TO MOUNT aye aye sir* hallowed be Thy name *MOUNT!* Thy kingdom come, if I die on the Russian front bury me with a Russian cunt *DO IT! DO IT! DO IT! DO IT!* Thy will be done *DO IT! DO IT! DO IT IN YOUR SLEEP ON THE FLOOR ON YOUR HEAD DO IT NOW WANT TO BE-COME MEN WANT TO BECOME MEN WANT TO BECOME MEN oh, become, marines oh god bless*

the marine corps god bless america TIGHTEN UP!
TIGHTEN UP! *god bless my senior drill instruc-
tor god bless the president* PLATOON HALT! *god
bless the battalion commander god bless chesty
puller god bless john wayne* From the halls of Mon-
tezuma BY THE RIGHT FLANK! AWRIGHT
WHEN I TELL YOU PEOPLE YOU GOT TWO
FUCKIN MINUTES TO SHIT SHOWER AND
SHAVE I MEAN EXACTLY THAT NOW GET
DOWN SCUMBAGS! MAIL CALL! *(eighty chests
hitting the deck) i want the flag* SECOND'S AS
GOOD AS LAST LADIES! *can't you see, Father,
the tests in spring shots* GOTTA BE FIRST
GOTTA BE FIRST! STARBOARD SIDE MAKE A
HEAD CALL PORTSIDE MAKE A HEAD CALL
oh hail Mary full of grace the Lord is *motherfuck-
ing cocksuckers!* oh Our Father KILL! KILL!
KILL! KILL! Who art in COMMIES CHINKS JAPS
AND DINKS hallowed be IF YOU WANT TO BE
MARINES . . . HAVE TO PAY THE PRICE PAY
THE PRICE PAY THE PRICE If I die in a combat
zone box me up and ship me home, Thy kingdom
come *private kovic sir two-oh-three-oh-two-six-one
sir yessir no sir one two aye aye sir* Thy will be
done *the private requests permission to speak to his
senior drill instructor oh god oh jesus help me help
me* on earth as it is in heaven SCHOOL CIRCLES!
aye aye sir as it is WHAT DO YOU WANT MAG-
GOT? READY—SEATS! *aye aye sir* DO IT! *aye
aye sir* THIS IS YOUR RIFLE I WANT YOU TO
SLEEP WITH IT GET UP GET DOWN GET UP
GET DOWN DO YOU HEAR ME? DO YOU HEAR
ME PEOPLE? *(we are moving now)* GET OUT OF

*THE PASSAGEWAY GIMME FIVE HUNDRED
BENDS AND THRUSTS aye aye sir one two aye
aye sir one two DON'T STOP PEOPLE KEEP
RUNNING PEOPLE SCUM SCUM SWINE
SWINE THERE WILL BE NO DROPOUTS TO-
DAY THERE WILL BE NO QUITTERS IN MY
MARINE CORPS! RUN! RUN! RUN! RUN! YOU
BETTER BE DEAD IF YOU DROP OUT* There is
nothing finer *QUICKLY! QUICKLY! and when i
grow up i'm going to TEN!NINE!EIGHT!SEVEN!-
SIX!FIVE!FOUR!THREE!TWO!ONE!   YOU'RE
LATE! LATE LATE LATE LATE LATE LATE!
(raising the flag) DON'T MOVE DON'T SIT
DON'T STAND DO IT DO IT DO IT DO IT! FOR-
WARD—MARCH! o mary mother of jesus you
gotta help me WE ARE THE BEST WE ARE THE
BEST WE ARE THE BEST platoon one eighty-one
is the best KILL THEM AT THREE HUNDRED
FEET! DRESS RIGHT! AT THIRTY FEET! in the
trenches on the benches in the butts o get me outta
here god (cracking strings and pasting holes and
making hits) i'm an expert mom i'm an expert! oh
make this time this time i want to scream i want
to scream oh no oh wait, hey i'm, wait, i'm just,
wait i'm just going to screamscreamscreamscream
screamscreamscreamscreamscream   GOTTA
GRADUATE GOTTA GRADUATE! BY THE LEFT
FLANK—MARCH! YOU'LL NEVER MAKE IT!
BY THE RIGHT FLANK EIGHTY PLATOON ONE
EIGHTY! platoon one eighty-one sir! the colors
guidons guide posts guide posts oh god goal posts
touchdown touchdown jackets green utility's fresh
smell   one-two-three-four-one-two-three-four   (his*

voice the voices they them letters) hi mom and hi dad! MARINE CORPS MARINE CORPS MARINE CORPS PORK CHOP HILL From the halls of Montezuma *the vice president of the united states is* WE HAVE NEVER LOST! EMPTY THOSE SEA BAGS! I WANT YOU TO CRAWL WORMS CRAWL WORMS CRAWL! GET THOSE LOCKER BOXES ABOVE YOUR HEADS! WE HAVE NEVER LOST! *(tear apart racks tear apart racks)* YOU'RE EITHER GONNA SINK OR SWIM PEOPLE! LOOK STRAIGHT AHEAD LOOK STRAIGHT AHEAD! RUN!RUN!RUN!RUN!RUN! RUN!RUN!RUN!!!

4

THEY CAME FOR him early that morning, walking up the wooden ramp and knocking on the front door of his house. He could hear them in the living room talking to his mom and dad about the parade and how important it was to have him marching with them on Memorial Day in his wheelchair.

"Parade time," his father said, walking into his room.

"I'll be right with you, Dad," he said, looking up from his bed. "I've got to get my pants on."

It was always hard getting dressed, but he was getting better at it. He turned from his back to his stomach, grabbing his pants and pulling them up until they reached his waist. Turning on his back again, he buckled his belt. Then he pushed himself with both hands in back of him until he was sitting up in the bed next to his wheelchair. He grabbed the chair with one hand, dragging his body across in a quick sweeping motion until he was seated, his legs still up on the bed.

Now his father knew it was time to help. He took each leg, carefully lowering them one at a time to the chair, spreading them apart to make sure the rubber tube wasn't twisted.

"Ready?" shouted the boy.

"Ready!" said his dad. And his father went in back of the chair as he always did and lifted him up underneath his arms so that he could pull his pants up again.

"Good," said the boy.

His father let him slowly down back onto the cushion and he turned around in his wheelchair to face the door and pushed his chair down the long, narrow hallway to the living room. His mom was there with a tall man he immediately remembered from the hospital; right next to him was a heavy guy. Both of them had on their American Legion uniforms with special caps placed smartly on their heads. He sat as straight in his chair as he could, holding on with one hand so he wouldn't lose his balance. He shook hands with the tall commander and with the heavy guy who stood beside him.

"You sure look great," said the tall commander, stepping forward. "Same tough marine we visited in the hospital," he said, smiling, "You know, Mr. Kovic—" he was looking at his father now— "this kid of yours sure has a lot of guts."

"We're really proud of him," said the heavy guy.

"The whole town's proud of him and what he did," said the tall commander, smiling again.

"He's sacrificed a lot," said the heavy guy, putting his hand on the boy's shoulder.

"And we're gonna make certain," the tall commander said, "we're gonna make certain that his sacrifice and any of the others weren't in vain. We're still in that war to win," he said, looking at the boy's father. His father nodded his head up and down, showing the commander he understood.

It was time to go. The heavy guy had grabbed the back handles of the chair. Acting very confident, he reminded the boy that he had worked in the naval hospital.

The boy said goodbye to his mom and dad, and the heavy guy eased the wheelchair down the long wooden ramp to the sidewalk in front of the house. "I've been pushin' you boys around for almost two years now," he said.

The boy listened as the heavy guy and the commander stood for a moment in the front yard trying to figure out how they were going to get him into the back seat of the Cadillac convertible.

"You're goin' in style today," shouted the commander.

"Nothing but the best," said the heavy guy.

"I haven't learned how to . . ."

"We know, we understand," said the commander.

And before he could say another word, the heavy guy who had worked at the hospital lifted him out of the chair in one smooth motion. Opening the door with a kick of his foot, he carefully placed him in the back seat of the big open car.

"All right, Mr. Grand Marshal." The heavy guy patted him on the shoulder, then jumped into the car with the commander, beeping the horn all the way down Toronto Avenue.

"We're goin' over to Eddie Dugan's house," said the commander, turning his head. "Ya know Eddie?" He was talking very fast now. "Good boy," said the commander. "Lost both legs like you. Got plastic ones. Doin' great, isn't he?" He jabbed the heavy man with his fist.

"Got a lot of guts that kid Eddie Dugan," the heavy man said.

"I remember him . . ." The commander was turning the corner now, driving slowly down the street. "Yeah, I remember Eddie way back when he was . . . when he was playin' on the Little Leagues. And as God is my witness," said the commander, turning his head back toward him again, "as God is my witness, I seen Eddie hit a home run on his birthday. He was nine or ten, something like that back then." The commander was laughing now. "I was coaching with his dad and it was Eddie's birthday. A lot of you guys got messed up over there." He was still talking very fast.

"Remember Clasternack? You heard of Clasternack, didn't you? He got killed. They got a street over in the park named after him." He paused for a long time. "Yeah . . . he got killed. He was the first of you kids to get it. And there were others too," said the commander. "That little guy, what was his name? Yeah I got it . . . Johnny Heanon . . . little Johnny Heanon . . . he used to play in the Little League with you guys."

He remembered Johnny Heanon.

"He tripped a land mine or something and died on the hospital ship during the operation. I see his folks every once in a while. They live down by the old high school. Fine kid," said the commander.

"He used to deliver my paper," said the heavy guy.

"There was the Peters family too . . . both brothers, . . ." said the commander again, pausing for a long time. "Both of them got killed in the same week. And Alan Grady. . . . Did you know Alan Grady? He used to go to the boy scouts when you kids was growing up."

The boy in the back seat nodded. He knew Alan Grady too.

"He drowned," said the commander.

"Funny thing," said the heavy guy. "I mean, terrible way to go. He was on R and R or something and he drowned one afternoon when he was swimming."

"And Billy Morris," said the commander, "he used to get in all sorts of trouble down at the high school. He got killed too. There was a land mine or something and he got hit in the head with a tree. Isn't that crazy?" The commander was laughing almost hysterically now.

"He goes all the way over there and gets killed by a fucking tree."

"We've lost a lot of good boys," the heavy guy said. "We've been hit pretty bad. The whole town's changed."

"And it's been goin' on a long time." The commander was very angry now. "If those bastards in Washington would stop fiddlefucking around and drop a couple of big ones in the right places, we could get that whole thing over with next week. We could win that goddamn thing and get all our kids out of there."

When they got to Eddie Dugan's house, both of the men got out, leaving him in the back seat, and ran up to Eddie's doorstep. A few minutes passed, then Eddie came out the front door rocking back and forth across the lawn like a clown on his crutches until he had worked himself to the car door.

"I can do it," Eddie said.

"Sure," said the tall commander, smiling.

They watched as Eddie stretched leaning on his crutches, then swung into the car seat.

"Not bad," said the commander.

The commander and the heavy guy jumped back into the car and the boy could feel the warm spring air blowing on his face as they moved down Eddie's block. The leaves on the trees had blossomed full. They glistened in the sun, covering the streets in patches of morning shadow.

"You're not going to believe this," Eddie said to him, looking down at his legs. "I got hit by our own mortars." He was almost laughing now. "It was on a night patrol. . . . And you?" he asked.

"I got paralyzed from the chest down. I can't move or feel anything." He showed Eddie with his hand how far up he could not feel and then showed him the bag on the side of his leg. Usually he didn't like telling people how bad he had been hurt, but for some reason it was different with Eddie.

Eddie looked at the bag and shook his head, saying nothing.

"Let me see your new legs," he said to Eddie.

Eddie pulled up his trousers, showing his new plastic legs. "You see," he said, tapping them with his knuckles. He was very sarcastic. "As good as new."

They got to the place where the march was to begin and he saw the cub scouts and the girl scouts, the marching bands, the fathers in their Legion caps and uniforms, the mothers from the Legion's auxilliary, the pretty drum majorettes. The street was a sea of red, white, and blue. He remembered how he and all the rest of the kids on the block had put on their cub scout uniforms and marched every Memorial Day down these same streets. He remembered the hundreds of people lining the sidewalks, everyone standing and cheering and waving their small flags, his mother standing with the other mothers on the block shouting for him to keep in step. "There's my Yankee Doodle boy!" he'd hear her shouting, and he'd feel embarrassed, pulling his cap over his eyes like he always did.

There were scouts decorating the Cadillac now with red, white, and blue crepe paper and long paper banners that read WELCOME HOME RON KOVIC AND EDDIE DUGAN and SUPPORT OUR BOYS in VIETNAM. There was a small sign, too, that

read: OUR WOUNDED VIETNAM VETS . . . EDDIE
DUGAN AND RON KOVIC.

When the scouts were finished, the commander
came running over to the car with a can of beer
in his hand. "Let's go!" he shouted, jumping back
in with the heavy guy.

They drove slowly through the crowd until they
were all the way up in the front of the parade. He
could hear the horns and drums behind him and
he looked out and watched the pretty drum majorettes and clowns dancing in the street. He
looked out onto the sidewalks where the people
from his town had gathered just like when he was
a kid.

But it was different. He couldn't tell at first exactly what it was, but something was not the
same, they weren't waving and they just seemed
to be standing staring at Eddie Dugan and himself like they weren't even there. It was as if they
were ghosts like little Johnny Heanon or Billy
Morris come back from the dead. And he couldn't
understand what was happening.

Maybe, he thought, the banners, the ones the
boy scouts and their fathers had put up, the ones
telling the whole town who Eddie Dugan and he
were, maybe, he thought, they had dropped off
into the street and no one knew who they were
and that's why no one was waving.

If the signs had been there, they'd have been
flooding into the streets, stomping their feet and
screaming and cheering the way they did for him
and Eddie at the Little League games. They'd have
been swelling into the streets, trying to shake

their hands just like in the movies, when the boys
had come home from the other wars and everyone
went crazy throwing streamers of paper and con-
fetti and hugging their sweethearts, sweeping
them off their feet and kissing them for what
seemed forever. If they really knew who they
were, he thought, they'd be roaring and clapping
and shouting. But they were quiet and all he heard
whenever the band stopped playing was the soft
purr of the American Legion's big Cadillac as it
moved slowly down the street.

Even though it seemed very difficult acting like
heroes, he and Eddie tried waving a couple of
times, but after a while he realized that the staring faces weren't going to change and he couldn't
help but feel like he was some kind of animal in
a zoo or that he and Eddie were on display in
some trophy case. And the more he thought about
it, the more he wanted to get the hell out of the
back seat of the Cadillac and go back home to his
room where he knew it was safe and warm. The
parade had hardly begun but already he felt
trapped, just like in the hospital.

The tall commander turned down Broadway
now, past Sparky the barber's place, then down to
Massapequa Avenue, past the American Legion
hall where the cannon they had played on as kids
sat right across from the Long Island Railroad
station. He thought of the times he and Bobby
and Richie Castiglia used to sit on that thing with
their plastic machine guns and army-navy store
canteens full of lemonade; they'd sit and wait until
a train pulled into the Massapequa station, and

then they'd all scream "Ambush!" with Castiglia standing up bravely on the cannon barrel, riddling the train's windows.

He was beginning to feel very lonely. He kept looking over at Eddie. Why hadn't they waved, he thought. Eddie had lost both of his legs and he had come home with almost no body left, and no one seemed to care.

When they came to where the speakers' platform had been erected, he watched Eddie push himself out of the back seat, then up on his crutches while the heavy guy helped him with the door. The commander was opening the trunk, bringing the wheelchair to the side of the car. He was lifted out by the heavy guy and he saw the people around him watching, and it bothered him because he didn't want them to see how badly he had been hurt and how helpless he was, having to be carried out of the car into the chair like a baby. He tried to block out what he was feeling by smiling and waving to the people around him, making jokes about the chair to ease the tension, but it was very difficult being there at all and the more he felt stared at and gawked at like some strange object in a museum, the more difficult it became and the more he wanted to get the hell out of there.

He pushed himself to the back of the platform where two strong members of the Legion were waiting to lift him up in the chair. "How do you lift this goddamn thing?" shouted one of the men, suddenly staggering, almost dropping him. He tried to tell them how to lift it properly, the way they had shown him in the hospital, but they wanted to do it their own way and almost dropped him a second time.

They finally carried him up the steps of the stage where he was wheeled up front next to Eddie, who sat with his crutches by his side. They sat together watching the big crowd and listening to one speaker after the other, including the mayor and all the town's dignitaries; each one spoke very beautiful words about *sacrifice and patriotism and God,* crying out to the crowd to support the boys in the war so that their brave sacrifices would not have to be in vain.

And then it was the tall commander's turn to speak. He walked up to the microphone slowly, measuring his steps carefully, then jutted his head up and looked directly at the crowd. *"I believe in America!"* shouted the commander, shaking his fist in the air. *"And I believe in Americanism!"* The crowd was cheering now. *"And most of all . . . most of all, I believe in victory for America!"* He was very emotional. Then he shouted that the whole country had to come together and support the boys in the war. He told how he and the boys' fathers before them had fought in Korea and World War II, and how the whole country had been behind them back then and how they had won a great victory for freedom. Almost crying now, he shouted to the crowd that they couldn't give up in Vietnam. *"We have to win . . ."* he said, his voice still shaking; then pausing, he pointed his finger at him and Eddie Dugan, *". . . because of them!"*

Suddenly it was very quiet and he could feel them looking right at him, sitting there in his wheelchair with Eddie all alone. It seemed everyone—the cub scouts, the boy scouts, the mothers, the fathers, the whole town—had their eyes on them and now he bent his head and stared into his lap.

The commander left the podium to great applause and the speeches continued, but the more they spoke, the more restless and uncomfortable he became, until he felt like he was going to jump out of his paralyzed body and scream. He was confused, then proud, then all of a sudden confused again. He wanted to listen and believe everything they were saying, but he kept thinking of all the things that had happened that day and now he wondered why he and Eddie hadn't even been given the chance to speak. They had just sat there all day long, like he had been sitting in his chair for weeks and months in the hospital and at home in his room alone, and he wondered now why he had allowed them to make him a hero and the grand marshal of the parade with Eddie, why he had let them take him all over town in that Cadillac when they hadn't even asked him to speak.

These people had never been to his war, and they had been talking like they knew everything, like they were experts on the whole goddamn thing, like he and Eddie didn't know how to speak for themselves because there was something wrong now with both of them. They couldn't speak because of the war and had to have others define for them with their lovely words what they didn't know anything about.

He sat back, watching the men who ran the town as they walked back and forth on the speakers' platform in their suits and ties, drinking their beer and talking about patriotism. It reminded him of the time in church a few Sundays before, when Father Bradley had suddenly pointed to him during the middle of the sermon, telling everyone he was a hero and a patriot in the eyes of God and his country for going to fight the Communists. "We must pray for brave boys like Ron Kovic," said the priest. "And most of all," he said, "we must pray for victory in Vietnam and peace throughout the world." And when the service was over, people came to shake his hand and thank him for all he had done for God and his country, and he left the church feeling very sick and threw up in the parking lot.

After all the speeches, they carried him back down the steps of the platform and the crowd started clapping and now he felt more embarrassed than ever. He didn't deserve this, he didn't want this shit. All he could think of was getting out of there and going back home. He just wanted to get out of this place and go back right away.

But now someone in the crowd was calling his name. "Ronnie! Ronnie!" Over and over again he heard someone shouting. And finally he saw who it was. It was little Tommy Law, who had grown up on Hamilton Avenue with all the rest of the guys. He used to hit home runs over Tommy's hedge. Tommy had been one of his best friends

like Richie and Bobby Zimmer. He hadn't seen
him for years, not since high school. Tommy had
joined the marines too, and he'd heard something
about him being wounded in a rocket attack in
the DMZ. No one had told him he was back from
the war. And now Tommy was hugging him and
they were crying, both of them at the bottom of
the stage, hugging each other and crying in front
of all of them that day. He wanted to pull away
in embarrassment and hold back his feelings that
seemed to be pouring out of him, but he could not
and he cried even harder now, hugging his friend
until he felt his arms go numb. It was so wonderful, so good, to see Tommy again. He seemed to
bring back something wonderfully happy in his
past and he didn't want to let go. They held on to
each other for a long time. And when Tommy
finally pulled away, his face was bright red and
covered with tears and pain. Tommy held his
head with his hands still shaking, looking at him
sitting there in disbelief. He looked up at Tommy's
face and he could see that he was very sad.

The crowd had gathered now watching the two
friends almost with curiosity. He tried wiping the
tears from his eyes, still trying to laugh and make
Tommy and himself and all the others feel more
at ease, but Tommy would not smile and he kept
holding his head. Still crying, he shook his head
back and forth. And now, looking up at Tommy's
face, he could see the thin scar that ran along his
hairline, the same kind of scar he'd seen on the
heads of the vegetables who had had their brains

blown out, where plates had been put in to re-place part of the skull.

But Tommy didn't want to talk about what had happened to him. "Let's get out of here," he said. He grabbed the back handles of the chair and be-gan pushing him through the crowd. He pushed him through the town past the Long Island Rail-road station to the American Legion hall. They sat in the corner of the bar, watching the mayor and all the politicians. And Tommy tried to keep the drunken Legion members from hanging all over him and telling him their war stories.

The tall commander, who was now very drunk, came over asking Tommy and him if they wanted a ride back home in the Cadillac. Tommy said they were walking home, and they left the Amer-ican Legion hall and the drunks in the bar, with Tommy pushing his wheelchair, walking back through the town where they had grown up, past the baseball field at Parkside School where they had played as kids, back to Hamilton Avenue, where they sat together in front of Peter Weber's house almost all night, still not believing they were together again.

I AM WATCHING THE young couple walk along the beach. They are walking on the wet sand just where the waves wash up to the shore. The girl is holding his hand and she is laughing. Oh I want so badly to be that guy with her. I want to feel, I want to feel again, I want to walk with a woman, I want to be just like that guy who is walking with her along the beach. Please God, I say, I want it back so bad. I will give anything, anything, just to be inside a woman again. I think of approaching them. It would be so difficult. What could I say? "Excuse me, would you like to pull my chair across the sand? Or maybe you'd like to carry me over your shoulders and I could hold your hand laughing . . ." NO NO NO NO, that's not right! That's not fair! I want it back! They have taken it, they have robbed it, my penis will never get hard anymore. I didn't even have time to learn how to enjoy it and now it is gone, it is dead, it is as numb as the rest of me.

I watch the other women now. I see their long

slim legs standing pretty. I start to get excited, my mind racing with fantasies, and then the hurt comes. . . .

Oh God, I never dreamed that this could possibly happen, that this part of me that had made me feel so good when I was young, that this wonderful thing that no one ever seems to want to talk about . . . has gone, has suddenly disappeared. It has happened so fast, so quickly. What can I do, how can I ever get it back? Everyone says it is such an important thing, but nobody wants to talk about it. The Church says if you play with it, it is a sin. Now I can't even roll on top of a basketball, I can't do it in the bathtub or against the tree in the yard. It is over with. Gone. And it is gone for America. I have given it for democracy. It is okay now. It is all right. Yes it is all right. I have given my dead swinging dick for America. I have given my numb young dick for democracy. It is gone and numb, lost somewhere out there by the river where the artillery is screaming in. Oh God oh God I want it back! I gave it for the whole country, I gave it for every one of them. Yes, I gave my dead dick for John Wayne and Howdy Doody, for Castiglia and Sparky the barber. Nobody ever told me I was going to come back from this war without a penis. But I am back and my head is screaming now and I don't know what to do.

Every night after he had been to Arthur's Bar, he would push up his old man's wooden ramp. He would stop at the top in his chair, knocking the big blue milk can into the bushes, cursing under his breath and opening the screen door that his old man would leave unbolted. It was always two or three in the morning by then and he would try to slip into the house without waking anybody even though he could barely push the chair. Every night he stopped next to the crucifix and stuck his fingers into the holy water. Oh Jesus, he mumbled to himself, you gotta help me, you gotta find me a woman, someone to love this broken body of mine. He would make the sign of the cross with the holy water just as he had done when he was a kid. Oh Jesus, please Jesus, you gotta help me, you gotta give me strength. This broken body ain't gonna mend and it's gonna be this way for a long time and you gotta help me now Jesus you gotta help me somehow. Sometimes the dog would come up to him and he would tap it softly on the head. Well, here's a real friend, someone I can count on. He would turn the chair and push it down the narrow hallway, past the bookshelf, banging his hand against the wall, cursing, then pushing the chair angrily into his room. He would stay up all night sometimes, sitting by the typewriter, trying to forget the war, the wound, by putting words down on paper.

> there was a soldier
> tapdancing softly in the rain
> above the coffin
> six feet above, the people praying

They had to carry him out of Arthur's Bar one

night. The people were still dancing and the band was blasting really loud and he was screaming. There was a girl. He wanted to dance with her and squeeze her, kiss her soft face and take her home. *Here, don't worry about the chair, we can leave it here, we can go to your apartment and I can take your clothes off. I can lie with you and stroke your long slim body. I can kiss you and make love to you. We can make babies and I can tell you about the war. We can make lots of babies.*

He was very drunk, drunker than he had ever been. The whole place was spinning and it became very hard to hear anything but a great rushing sound that roared in his ears like a terrific storm. "You got to get out of here," they were telling him. "You got to get in the car and go home." They slowly lifted the body into the small car. He was laughing now, laughing and singing Irish songs. "Hurry up now," he could hear them saying. "Hurry up now and we'll get you back home." They all seemed to look like funny cartoon characters moving the numb limbs of his lower part into the front seat of the car. "That's right, that's good now," they were saying. Some girl was laughing in the back seat and the driver told her to shut up. "Are you okay, is everything all right?" said his friend.

"He's really drunk, really smashed," said the girl. "We got to get him home right away."

"How are his legs? Are his legs okay?"

The rubber urine bag. He moved his hand slowly down his leg to the rubber urine bag. It was as hard as a rock and his pants were soaked and it was all slowly soaking into the seat.

"He's pissed all over the fucking seat," said the girl. "What should we do?"

"Get him home. Drop him off."

They got him to the house and lifted him out into his chair and there was the front seat of the car all soaked. It was very late and the young girl almost seemed in a panic. The two boys pushed him up the wooden ramp his father had built with his own hands. He had put it all together just before he came home from the hospital. His old man had worked long and hard on the ramp to make it just right for his son who had just come home from the war. It was a piece of art, just like the special room with the shower. Every piece had been cut to fit and there were two long smooth handrails. The whole thing was painted red like the house. The old man had worked hard on the ramp, like he had worked hard in the food store for twenty-five years, like he worked hard at everything he ever did in his life.

His mother screamed when he came in. She was still screaming hysterically when the old man bent down and lifted him up onto the little bed. He laid the body gently down and began to hook up the plastic tube. Then he took the piss-soaked pants off and undid the rocklike rubber piss bag from his boy's leg.

"I'm fucked up, I'm fucked up," the boy was saying.

His mother went racing in and out of the room.

"He's drunk, he's drunk," she repeated to the old man. "We've got a drunk for a son."

The old man didn't seem to hear her. He grabbed a warm washcloth and began scrubbing his son. The last thing he did was to connect the rubber tube that went into the boy's penis to the long plastic tube that went into the bag on the side of the bed. That was what the nurses in the hospital had taught him to do. It was very important to connect the rubber tube in the boy's penis to the plastic tube when he went to bed at night. So that everything would run okay. So that everything would be all right. So he did it just the way they had told them and after pulling the sheets and covers up over the body and just below the shoulders of his son, the old man walked out of the room.

The lights went out in the house. The boy turned slowly over until he had propped himself up on both elbows with his head pushed down into his pillow. He wanted to forget the terrible night. He wanted to forget it and everything else, the numb legs, the unfeeling numbness. He was lost, more lost than he had ever been in his life. Lost in some kind of limbo land of the dead. He wanted to explode, to get out of this crazy numb body and be a man again. He wanted to be free again, to walk in his back yard on the grass. He wanted to run down to Sparky's and get a haircut, he wanted to play stickball with Richie, to swing the bat, to feel the gravel on Hamilton Avenue beneath his feet again. He wanted to stand up in the shower every morning with the hot water streaming down his back and off his legs.

It was now very clear that this thing was final like death.

No one, he thought, ever wanted to think about final things, dead things, things that ended abruptly or could not be explained. Once someone died, he thought, people just put them in the ground, they put them in the ground and stood above the grave saying words that helped explain why there was an end to the person, words that were beautiful like the flowers and the big stone, words that helped others realize that it wasn't the end, but only the beginning of a wonderful thing. It was so easy for them to say the words, to deny the finality. Why weren't they saying the words over his bed? Why weren't they telling him that this whole thing, this whole crazy numb thing, wasn't final? But for him there were no words and no people, nothing to tell him things would be beautiful again. This end was no beginning. It was starting to become very clear that there would be no change in his condition, no reconciliation with the half of his body that seemed so utterly lost forever. He was in the rain, trapped, and there was no one. It was ugly and cold and final.

HE WATCHED THE island disappear as the plane took off from Kennedy Airport. For the first time since he had come home from the war, he was getting away, going off somewhere by himself. His chair was safely packed in the belly of the plane, and he was just one of the other passengers, sitting there just like everybody else. Sometimes when he was out in his car, driving around, cruising up and down the block and into the town with his hand controls, he would get the same kind of feeling. It was a really free feeling that he couldn't get unless he was out of the chair.

He had been thinking about going to Mexico for a long time. In the hospital there had been a brochure that said there was this place down there where people like himself were cared for. It was a place called the Village of the Sun. He'd even met one guy who'd been there and talked about a whorehouse he'd gone to where the whores were very understanding, where even paralyzed men could get fucked. He thought about the Village of the Sun all the time after that. He just knew inside he could make love again, even though all the parts had been destroyed by the war.

It was night by the time he arrived in Guadalajara. A man named Rahilio met him at the airport and put him in his Ford pickup. It had been a long trip and now it was going to be a long ride to Las Fuentes and the Village, but he was happy to be in Mexico. Rahilio's small son lay on the seat next to him singing a song he couldn't understand. He opened up his window and looked out into the dark Mexican countryside.

The long dining hall full of wheelchairs was an exciting place for him the next morning. There were a lot of people talking and laughing and the sun was very bright on the white walls and the colorful tile tables. There were old and young, veterans from all the wars. Aides ran back and forth helping the men who couldn't use their hands to eat. It made him feel good to be with so many others who were like himself. He felt accepted here. He thought he might be able to feel human again.

It was the Fourth of July and that night after dinner Rahilio's wife came up to him with a big cake and everybody began to sing "Happy Birthday." Somehow they had found out it was his birthday.

He could see you could have a nice life here if you wanted to. Some of the veterans he met were planning to stay at the Village of the Sun until

they died. He could see there were a lot of reasons
not to go back to the States again. A lot of the
men would play cards all day long and some
would drink heavily and have to be carried back
into their rooms. They got pretty loud during the
card games with their women hanging over their
shoulders, big-busted Mexican women. It was
something you would never see back home. Some
of the others just stayed in their little rooms writing letters to people or reading the newspaper.

It was a week before he got really restless, before he got tired of sitting around the Village. It
was a Sunday and he asked Rahilio if he could
go to church with him and his children. It was
very quiet in the little Spanish chapel, the men
sitting on one side and the women on the other.
He listened to the small birds that flew above
the altar during the Mass, chirping and singing.
After church he told Rahilio he wanted to go into
the city.

He was lonely and he wanted to move around.
. . . He had come almost three thousand miles
and now, finally, he was riding in a cab and
maybe in one of the houses in the city he was
going to find a woman like the women they had
told him about, a woman who would love him
and make his broken body come alive again, who
would lie down next to the disfigurement and
love it like there was not anything the matter
with him at all. He cried inside for a woman, any
woman, to lie close to him. In the hospital there
were so many times when he had looked at the

nurses and all the visitors and it would seem so crazy that the same government that provided a big check for the wounded men couldn't provide someone warm, someone who cared for him.

The cabdriver left him off at the Hilton Hotel. For a long time after that he had lunch there every day. After lunch he would wheel all over the city, taking cabs and pushing the chair as far as he could until his arms began to ache. There would always be people to help him up and down the big Mexican curbs. There were beautiful cathedrals and statues everywhere he looked, and the sky was clear most of the time.

Finally one afternoon he went up to the guy who worked behind the desk at the Hilton and asked him where the biggest whorehouse in town was. The guy behind the desk wrote down the address for him and he wheeled out to the street and caught a cab.

The girl was very beautiful and the jukebox was playing as she pushed his chair into the small room. There was an old mattress on the floor and he got himself onto it and began to take his shirt off, watching the girl as she took off all her clothing. She lay down in the bed next to him and asked him why he wasn't taking off his pants.

"I can't." He hesitated. It was very hard for him to talk about. "I can't take them off," he said. He pointed to his legs. "They were paralyzed in the war."

She looked at him and seemed very confused.

"The war," he said. "Vietnam. Have you ever heard of Vietnam?"

"Vietnam, yes."

"I can't move it," he said, showing her his penis. "You see this?" he said, pointing at the yellow catheter tube. "It doesn't move anymore and I have to use this tube. You see this tube," he said, pointing to it again. "It's okay," he said. "Don't worry about it, *senorita* is *muy bonita*," he said, staring at her dark eyes. "We can still love," he said.

The tears began to roll down her face. She was sitting in the bed next to him crying.

"You see?" he said, pointing to the scar on his chest. "This is where they stuck a chest tube. . . ."

She was getting up now and putting her clothes back on. She was still crying. She was so very beautiful and he wanted so much to lie with her body warm and soft against the top of him, where he could still feel. But now she was walking out the door, leaving for good. She didn't even ask for his money, she didn't even want that.

He lay there for a long time until the madam came in and said it was time for him to leave. It was getting very late, she said. He put on his shirt and dragged his body across the bed, back into the wheelchair. The madam helped him out into the street.

It was early in the morning and the sun was about to come up and he sat crying outside the whorehouse. A cab came by. The driver stopped and asked him if he needed anything. "Do you need a woman?" he said. "Hey, want to go to a great whorehouse? There's a woman in there that will knock you out, really knows how to fuck."

There wasn't anything left to lose, he thought.

The driver got out of his cab and pushed him down the street to a place that was still open. "Wait a minute out here. I'll be right back," he told him. He came back with a big smile on his face. "Maria will be right out," he said, and pushed him into the bar.

A very young girl came into the room, walking past all the tables and then up to his. She had long brown hair down to her waist. "Do you want to sleep with me?" she said. He looked at her and said, "Yes." She seemed very excited, her brown eyes as bright as a little child's. He thanked the cabdriver and gave him some money and followed the girl into one of the tiny cubicles.

She was so much more relaxed than the other woman. He didn't have to explain anything to her. She lay down and touched his face gently. She kissed him and pushed her breasts next to his chest. She felt warm and good. She didn't seem to notice his pants were still on, or the catheter, the rubber urine bag, or any of that. She loved him, they loved each other on the bed in the little room, for what seemed a very long time. She didn't care about the war or any of the other things. They laughed and rolled on top of each other, hiding under the blankets, and talked about a lot of things. She told him she had a kid, a little girl, and they lived in the city. It was very lonely she told him and she really didn't want to do what she was doing, but it was the only way she could make money for herself and her baby. He held her in his arms as if she were his sister as well as his lover.

There was a loud knock on the door and the cabdriver yelled in a taunting voice that it was time for him to get out. But she laughed and said something in Spanish and they stayed in bed almost an extra ten minutes over the limit. When she was getting dressed she asked him if he wanted to get married. She told him she loved him very much and wrote down her address on a small piece of paper. "Here. You take this," she said. She helped him put on his shirt and buttoned each one of the buttons for him. "Come see me tomorrow at four," she said. "You can live with me. *Dinero*," she said, and he gave her fifteen dollars and she helped him into the chair.

All the way back to the village he thought about her and how they would live together and learn each other's language. He saw them sitting naked in bed together studying their books, the child playing at their feet. But then he began to think she hadn't really meant it and he didn't go back the next day at four. He went to a different place and lay with a different girl.

He went out almost every night after that, coming in every morning just after the sun came up and sleeping until four in the afternoon. Then he would get up and get ready to go into the city. Rahilio would call a cab for him and he would wait for it outside the gate of the Village of the Sun.

He would go from whorehouse to whorehouse, wheeling the chair in past the pretty painted Mexican women. He would find a table and wait for one to come up and talk to him. Usually they were kind and did not pity him. They would smile back, very interested, very curious, and he would smell their perfume and look at their breasts. He would sleep with a different one every night. He wanted to sleep with as many as he could, trying one after the other.

One night another Vietnam veteran from the Village came in with him, a guy named Charlie. Charlie had some good weed and said he wanted to have a real party. They got very stoned and very drunk together, and in the last whorehouse they went to Charlie got into a wild fight with one of the whores. He punched her in the face because she laughed at him when he pulled down his pants and told her he couldn't feel his penis or move it anymore. He was crazy drunk and he kept yelling and screaming, swinging his arms and his fists at the crowd who had gathered around him. "That goddamn fucking slut! I'm gonna kill that whore for ever laughing at me. That bitch thinks it's funny I can't move my dick. Fuck you! Fuck all of you goddamn mother-fuckers! They made me kill babies! They made me kill babies!" Charlie screamed again and again.

The owner was shaking his fist, telling them both to get out and never come back, and he knew someone was going to kill them if they didn't leave right away. But he just sat there in the middle of the bar, unable to move. What Charlie was saying was what he had been feeling for a long time.

Finally the owner got a couple of guys and threw them out into the street. They managed to get a cab, but halfway home Charlie got into another fight with the driver over the money he was charging, and they both had to get out in the middle of the highway.

They sat by the edge of the road for a long time until a Mexican truckdriver picked them up. He just picked them up as if there was nothing at all unusual about finding the two of them out there. He lifted them out of their chairs and put them into the cab of his truck. Charlie was singing by the time they got to the Village and had pissed all over the seat; the driver opened his window but never complained.

Somehow that was the end of it for him. The whole thing was over. He had a real cold feeling about it now. He didn't go back to the city the next night. He spent one more day in the Village, then told Rahilio he'd had enough. He caught the next plane back to New York.

IT IS THE END of the summer when I get back. The days are long and hot and there is still so much restlessness in me. I sit in my parents' living room and try to watch the baseball game on television. I keep going down to Arthur's Bar. I begin to think about getting an apartment. I have never lived alone, but I decide to try it now.

I get a place in Hempstead near the university. The rent is two hundred dollars, but I never think much about money anymore. I just spend the big checks I get from the government. I go all over Hempstead buying out the furniture stores. I buy an electric typewriter, a huge expensive stereo, a bunch of paintings. I don't care what things cost.

Every morning I wheel into the bathroom of my new apartment and throw up. It frightens me to live alone with my paralyzed body and my thoughts of Vietnam. I am dreaming too often of the dead corporal. The tension and fear are twisted up inside me like a loaded spring. I get into my car and drive around for hours. Sometimes I drive very fast.

I have registered at the university and it is much better when classes begin. Maybe all I needed was to be with people again. I begin to look back and think about the summer, about Mexico. Even with all the loneliness, there were times that had been good. My first summer without the war. I tell myself the war and the hospital are behind me now. The best years of my life are still ahead of me.

I am more determined than ever to learn to walk on braces and I exercise for hours every day. In the hospital they have shown me a way to stretch my legs a little and I am doing it one evening in my second week of school when I hear something snap. It sounds like the branch of a tree breaking off—and there is my right leg all twisted under me. I panic for the first few minutes, then call my father. He drives over right away and takes me to the hospital, the V.A. hospital in the Bronx. I spend the next six months there.

I am alone again. I have been lying in Room 17 for almost a month. I am isolated here because I am a troublemaker. I had a fight with the head nurse on the ward. I asked for a bath. I asked for the vomit to be wiped up from the floor. I asked to be treated like a human being.

My leg has swollen to twice its original size. The thigh bone had been completely shattered in the break, leaving the bone sticking out just beneath the surface of my skin. It sticks out like a knife and every few minutes my leg jumps in violent spasms, the bone cutting and stabbing back and forth. The big clumsy cast I have been encased in isn't doing any good. It is not going to heal. Again and again I wonder why it has happened, why I am back in the same place I fought so hard to leave before.

The doctor never seems to be around. When he does show up it is only for a minute to see if I am still alive. He walks in and out, mumbles a few words. Once he calls me by the wrong name. It frightens me.

It is like being in a prison. But it is not a prison, it is a hospital. The tall skinny man who brings my breakfast calls me Seventeen. "Seventeen!" he screams, waking me out of a doped sleep. "Seventeen! It's time to eat." Up and down the hall the nurses move like programmed robots, pushing their metal carts, giving shots, handing out medication. There is one nurse who always tells me I am crazy. She gives me extra doses of a drug to make me drowsy.

It is so easy to lose it all here. The whole place functions so smoothly, but somewhere along the way I am losing, and all the rest of the people whom I can't see in the rooms around me are losing too. Even if I make it out of this place, I think, even if I heal the leg, I will lose. No one ever leaves this place without losing something.

Early one morning the doctor comes into my room and tells me he's been thinking it might be a good idea to cut my leg off. He tells me that to cut the leg off would be a very simple thing. He makes it sound so easy, like there would be nothing to it. It's they who are all crazy in here, I think. They are all moving so quickly, all of them in such a fantastic hurry. This place is more like a factory to break people than to mend them and put them back together again. I don't want them to cut my leg off. It is numb and dead but it still means something to me. It is still mine. It is a part of me and I am not going to give it away that easily. Why isn't anyone helping me? I think over and over again. Why am I being forgotten in this place?

Something is happening to me in Room 17. I lie and stare at the walls of the small green box they have put me in. The walls are almost as dirty as the floor and I cannot even see out of the window. I feel myself changing, the anger is building up in me. It has become a force I cannot control. I push the call button again and again. No one comes. I am lying in my own excrement and no one comes. I begin shouting and screaming. I grab an ice pack and my water pitcher. I throw them out of the open door into the hallway, splashing water and ice all over the floor. I have been screaming for almost an hour when one of the aides walks by. He sticks his head in the door, taunting me and laughing. "I'm a Vietnam veteran," I tell him. "I fought in Vietnam and I've got a right to be treated decently."

"Vietnam," the aide says loudly. "Vietnam don't mean nothin' to me or any of these other people.

You can take your Vietnam and shove it up your ass."

I am in the intensive-care ward. It is so quiet I can hear the big round clock ticking on the green wall. There are mostly old men here. They are all attached to complicated machines. The clock keeps ticking. I look down. There are big stitches on my leg and two plastic tubes—one runs a clear fluid in and the other carries a bright red fluid back out of the wound. There is some kind of machine on the side of the bed that keeps clanking and pumping, keeping everything flowing nicely. I realize I have made it, I have lived through the operation. I am not going to die and they haven't cut my leg off. They have put a steel plate in. They have screwed in all the screws and sewn the whole thing up. I will be out of this place soon. The leg will heal and I will get out of this hospital. I will get out of it for good and never come back.

The pump stops suddenly. An aide comes over and kicks it. He curses at it and kicks it very hard. It still doesn't work, and I am frightened now that I will lose the leg. "Goddamn thing," he says. "This hospital doesn't ever have nothing but old equipment." He runs to look for a doctor.

The doctor who comes in isn't the one who did the operation. He is a younger man from a big university in the city. He tells me the pump is old and probably will not work anymore. "Well, doesn't this hospital have another one?" I say. "I can't believe that a modern veterans' hospital like this doesn't have an extra pump." The young doctor explains in a very matter-of-fact way that this is the only pump they have. It all has to do with the war, he explains. It is all because of the war. "The government is not giving us money for things that we need. It's really too bad. It's not fair at all."

"I've tried so hard to keep this leg," I tell him. "I've done everything. . . ." I'm trying to be calm, as calm as he is.

"Yes," he says, nodding his head. "I completely understand."

An hour or so later the pump starts going again. No one even kicks it. It just starts up by itself. They tell me I am very lucky.

The leg heals slowly. I am weak and sick for a long time, but I continue to survive in the Bronx V.A. hospital. There are times I scream and shout and throw things out my door. I get a bath and an enema every four days. I have to watch the pump all the time to make sure it doesn't stop. I am so tired, so weary. One day the doctor comes and pulls the two plastic tubes out of my leg and puts small bandages over the holes. He and an aide put me on a gurney and strap me down. They are very careful with my leg. I have two hospital canes and am able to push myself and the gurney up and down the hospital ward. It is the first freedom I have had in months and I am very careful not to go too fast.

I lie in the hall a lot. I do not talk to anyone. I am very quiet. My mother and father come down to see me every week. I do not even want to talk to them. I do not tell them what I have been thinking about the war and the wound and the hospital—that the whole thing is beginning to go round and round in my head. I am just beginning to see what it all adds up to. It would only hurt them if they knew.

I WAS IN VIETNAM when I first heard about the thousands of people protesting the war in the streets of America. I didn't want to believe it at first—people protesting against *us* when we were putting our lives on the line for our country. The men in my outfit used to talk about it a lot. How could they do this to us? Many of us would not be coming back and many others would be wounded or maimed. We swore they would pay, the hippies and draftcard burners. They would pay if we ever ran into them.

But the hospital had changed all that. It was the end of whatever belief I'd still had in what I'd done in Vietnam. Now I wanted to know what I had lost my legs for, why I and the others had gone at all. But it was still very hard for me to think of speaking out against the war, to think of joining those I'd once called traitors.

I settled into my apartment again and went back to classes at the university. It was the spring of 1970. I still wore a tie and sweater every day to school and had a short haircut. I was very sensitive to people looking at me in the wheelchair. I buried myself in my books, cutting myself off from the other students. It was as if they threatened me—particularly the activists, the radicals.

I was sitting alone in my apartment listening to the radio when I first heard the news about Kent State. Four students had just been shot in a demonstration against the invasion of Cambodia. For a moment there was a shock through my body. I felt like crying. The last time I had felt that way was the day Kennedy was killed. I remember saying to myself, The whole thing is coming down now. I wheeled out to my car. I didn't know where I was going but I had to find other people who felt the way I did. I drove down the street to the university. Students were congregating in small groups all over the place. The campus looked as if it were going to explode. Banners were going up and monitors with red armbands were walking up and down handing out leaflets. There was going to be a march and demonstration. I thought carefully for a moment or two, then decided to participate, driving my car past the hundreds of students marching down to the big parking lot where the rally was to be held. I honked my horn in support but I was still feeling a little hesitant. I stayed in my car all during the rally, listening intently to each speaker and cheering and shouting with the crowd. I was still acting like an observer. The last speaker was a woman who said there would be a huge rally in Washington that Saturday and that it was hoped that everyone would make it down. I decided I would go.

That night I called my cousin Ginny's husband Skip. He used to come and visit me at the hospital when I first came back and after I got out we became good friends. Sometimes we'd stay up all night at his house playing cards and talking about Vietnam and what had happened to me. Skip's views were very different from mine back then. He was against the war. And each time I left his house to go home, he'd give me books to read—books about the black people and poor people of the country. I laughed at him at first and didn't take the books too seriously, but it was lonely in my room and soon I began to read. And before long, every time I went to his house I asked for more books. Skip seemed surprised when I asked him to go to the rally with me but he said yes, and early Saturday morning we left for Washington.

The New Jersey Turnpike was packed with cars painted with flags and signs, and everywhere there were people hitching, holding up big cardboard peace symbols. You didn't have to ask where anyone was going. We were all going to the same place. Washington was a madhouse with buses and trucks and cars coming in from all directions.

We got a parking space and I gave up my tie and sweater for no shirt and a big red bandana around my head. Skip pushed the wheelchair for what seemed a mile or so. We could feel the tremendous tension. People were handing out leaflets reminding everyone that this was a nonviolent demonstration, and that no purpose would be served in violent confrontation. I remember feeling a little scared, the way I did before a firefight. After reading the leaflet I felt content that no one was going to get hurt.

Skip and I moved as close to the speakers' platform as we could and Skip lifted me out of my chair and laid me on my cushion. People were streaming into the Ellipse from all around us—an army of everyday people. There was a guy with a stereo tape deck blasting out music, and dogs running after Frisbees on the lawn. The Hari Krishna people started to dance and the whole thing seemed like a weird carnival. But there was a warmth to it, a feeling that we were all together in a very important place. A young girl sat down next to me and handed me a canteen of cool water. "Here," she said, "have a drink." I drank it down and passed it to Skip who passed it to someone else. That was the feeling that day. We all seemed to be sharing everything.

We listened as the speakers one after another denounced the invasion of Cambodia and the slaying of the students at Kent State. The sun was getting very hot and Skip and I decided to move around. We wanted to get to the White House where Nixon was holed up, probably watching television. We were in a great sea of people, thousands and thousands all around us. We finally made it to Lafayette Park. On the other side of the avenue the government had lined up thirty or

forty buses, making a huge wall between the people and the White House. I remember wondering
back then why they had to put all those buses in
front of the president. Was the government so
afraid of its own people that it needed such a
gigantic barricade? I'll always remember those
buses lined up that day and not being able to see
the White House from my wheelchair.

We went back to the rally for a while, then
went on down to the Reflecting Pool. Hundreds of
people had taken off their clothes. They were
jumping up and down to the beat of bongo drums
and metal cans. A man in his fifties had stripped
completely naked. Wearing only a crazy-looking
hat and a pair of enormous black glasses, he was
dancing on a platform in the middle of hundreds
of naked people. The crowd was clapping wildly.
Skip hesitated for a moment, then stripped all his
clothes off, jumping into the pool and joining the
rest of the people. I didn't know what all of this
had to do with the invasion of Cambodia or the
students slain at Kent State, but it was total freedom. As I sat there in my wheelchair at the edge
of the Reflecting Pool with everyone running
naked all around me and the clapping and the
drums resounding in my ears, I wanted to join
them. I wanted to take off my clothes like Skip
and the rest of them and wade into the pool and
rub my body with all those others. Everything
seemed to be hitting me all at once. One part of
me was upset that people were swimming naked
in the national monument and the other part of
me completely understood that now it was their

pool, and what good is a pool if you can't swim in it.

I remember how the police came later that day, very suddenly, when we were watching the sun go down—a blue legion of police in cars and on motorcycles and others with angry faces on big horses. A tall cop walked into the crowd near the Reflecting Pool and read something into a bull-horn no one could make out. The drums stopped and a few of the naked people began to put their clothes back on. It was almost evening and with most of the invading army's forces heading back along the Jersey Turnpike, the blue legion had decided to attack. And they did—wading their horses into the pool, flailing their clubs, smashing skulls. People were running everywhere as gas canisters began to pop. I couldn't understand why this was happening, why the police would attack the people, running them into the grass with their horses and beating them with their clubs. Two or three horses charged into the crowd at full gallop, driving the invading army into retreat toward the Lincoln Memorial. A girl was crying and scream-ing, trying to help her bleeding friend. She was yelling something about the pigs and kept step-ping backward away from the horses and the fly-ing clubs. For the first time that day I felt anger surge up inside me. I was no longer an observer, sitting in my car at the edge of a demonstration. I was right in the middle of it and it was ugly. Skip started pushing the chair as fast as he could up the path toward the Lincoln Memorial. I kept turning, looking back. I wanted to shout back at the charging police, tell them I was a veteran.

When we got to the memorial, I remember looking at Lincoln's face and reading the words carved on the walls in back of him. I felt certain that if he were alive he would be there with us.

I told Skip that I was never going to be the same. The demonstration had stirred something in my mind that would be there from now on. It was so very different from boot camp and fighting in the war. There was a togetherness, just as there had been in Vietnam, but it was a togetherness of a different kind of people and for a much different reason. In the war we were killing and maiming people. In Washington on that Saturday afternoon in May we were trying to heal them and set them free.

I<small>T</small> WILL BE *my turn to speak soon. They have put me up on the platform of this auditorium in this high school that is so much like the one I went to, in this town that is like the one I grew up in. I am looking at all the young faces. Kids. They were laughing, horsing around when they came in, just the way we used to. Now they are silent, looking at me and Bobby Muller, my friend from the V.A. hospital who is speaking to them from his wheelchair.*

It is like the day the marine recruiters came. I remember it like it was yesterday—their shiny shoes and their uniforms, their firm handshakes, all the dreams, the medals, the hills taken with Castiglia by my side his army-navy store canteen rattling, the movies the books the plastic guns, everything in 3-D and the explosive spiraling colors of a rainbow. Except this time, this time it is Bobby and me. What if I had seen someone like me that day, a guy in a wheelchair, just sitting there in front of the senior class not saying a word? Maybe things would have been different. Maybe that's all it would have taken.

Bobby is telling his story and I will tell mine. I am glad he has brought me here and that all of them are looking at us, seeing the war firsthand— the dead while still living, the living reminders, two young men who had the shit shot out of them.

I have never spoken before but it is time now. I am thinking about what I can tell them. I wheel myself to the center of the platform. I begin by telling them about the hospital.

5

AFTER THE SPEECH in the high school I spent less and less time going to classes at the university. Suddenly school no longer seemed important. What I really wanted to do was to go on speaking out. Bobby and I made a couple of other speeches at high schools together and once I did one by myself at a university. It was November and turning cold. Ever since I'd been wounded, I'd hated the cold weather. Snow was like a jailer for me. It made it so hard for me to get out of the house, to move around. I felt I'd stayed in one place for a very long time—I'd never lived more than a few miles from my parents' house except for the years when I was in Vietnam. For a while I thought of taking another trip to Mexico, but then just before Christmas my friend Kenny came home from California and asked me if I wanted to drive back across with him and live out there. I jumped at the idea of going. California seemed like such a warm and beautiful place, another planet. I cleaned my whole apartment out in one Sunday afternoon and gave all the furniture I owned to Mom and Dad. My car was packed that night and the next morning Kenny and I were on the road.

Three days later we'd gotten all the way to Texas. It was New Year's Eve. We celebrated it in a bar in Longview shooting a game of pool. The next day we got up early and drove straight through to Las Cruces, New Mexico. I remember big bramble bushes blowing in front of the car and dust all over everything. I wanted to push straight on to L.A., but Kenny and I hadn't eaten more than a few sandwiches in the last few days and we needed a good night's sleep. We stopped at a motel overnight and had a big breakfast of hot coffee and scrambled eggs before we started driving again. Even Kenny got excited later that afternoon when we passed the Great Salt Lake. He took the car the rest of the way in and I sat by the open window watching the orange groves and green trees begin to appear as we came out of the desert. It's California, I kept saying to myself, it's California. It got dark just as we came into L.A. and the lights went on all over the sprawling city like flickering little candles. No matter what Kenny or anybody said to me, this was Paradise, and like the pioneers before me I was going to make it my home. We got to Heliotrope Avenue and parked the car in front of Kenny's house. We went into his tiny apartment, turned the air conditioner on and fell asleep exhausted.

We rented a larger apartment down by the

ocean later that week, and after a while Kenny quit school. We hung out together all the time. It was so good to be with someone who'd known me all my life. Every day we went swimming with two girls who lived next door and Kenny bought himself a brand-new motorcycle. He strapped me on the back and took me riding on it the first day he brought it home.

I had been in California for about a month when one day there was a big photo on the front page of the *L.A. Times*—a group of vets had gone to Washington and thrown away their medals. It was one of the most moving antiwar demonstrations there had been. I would have given anything to have been there with them. I read about it sitting by the pool of the Santa Monica Bay Club, wearing a ridiculous Mickey Mouse shirt. Suddenly I knew my easy life could never be enough for me. The war had not ended. It was time for me to join forces with other vets.

I went home and called a couple of people I knew. One of them told me there was going to be a meeting of Vietnam Veterans Against the War that night in an apartment in L.A. I was still a bit unsure of myself but I couldn't wait to get into my car and drive over.

I remember how kind they were to me from the moment I arrived. When I got there, a bunch of vets were in front of the house waiting to carry me up the stairs in my chair. "Hi brother," they said to me warmly. "Can we help you brother? Is there anything we can do?"

All of a sudden everything seemed to change—

the loneliness seemed to vanish. I was surrounded by friends. They were the new veterans, the new soldiers with floppy bush hats and jungle uniforms right here on the streets of America. I began to feel closer to them than I ever had to the people at the university and at the hospital and all the people who had welcomed me back to Massapequa. It had a lot to do with what we had all been through. We could talk and laugh once again. We could be honest about the war and ourselves. Before each meeting there was the thumb-and-fist handshake—it meant you cared about your brother.

We were men who had gone to war. Each of us had his story to tell, his own nightmare. Each of us had been made cold by this thing. We wore ribbons and uniforms. We talked of death and atrocity to each other with unaccustomed gentleness.

I remember being very nervous and anxious at that first meeting. I told them, Give me a speech, give me a place to show this wheelchair. I really wanted to get going immediately. The brothers told me to calm down and not to worry, there would be plenty of chances to speak, it was time to get the organization together.

Afterward I went into the kitchen for a cup of coffee and one of the guys came up to me and gave me a big hug. He held me for a long time and when he let go there were tears streaming down his face. "I love you, brother," he said, wiping his eyes. And then he said, "I'm sorry, I'm really sorry I did that."

"It's okay," I said. "I love you too. Now when's my first speaking gig?"

They told me to go to a rally in Pasadena the next day. I would be speaking at noon with a couple of other people.

The VVAW sent me to do a lot of speeches after that and soon I was on television all the time. On one network there was a big argument with a producer who didn't want a disfigured veteran on her show. "We've seen enough of that," she told me over the phone. "Every night for the last couple of years people have seen it on the six o'clock news and they're tired of it." She tried to be nice and told me that she had read a book called *Johnny Got His Gun,* so she knew what I was all about, but she didn't think it would be tasteful at all to let the people of L.A. see a crippled kid on a Sunday morning.

I was at a rally a few weeks later when Donald Sutherland began to read the last couple of pages of the book the woman had talked to me about, the one about the kid in World War I who gets blown to hell like myself and loses almost everything, he's just a hulk, a slab of meat. Sutherland began to read the passage and something I will never forget swept over me. It was as if someone was speaking for everything I ever went through in the hospital. It was as if the book was speaking about me, my wound and the hell it had been coming back and learning to live with it. I began to shake and I remember there were tears in my eyes. Just before Sutherland was finished I found myself pushing my chair toward the stage and telling them that I wanted to be lifted up the steps. "I have a poem," I told them. "I have a poem I wrote about the vets who threw their medals away and I want to read it."

They broke all the rules and hoisted my chair up on the stage. I went up to the microphone and started reading. The crowd cheered when I was finished and again I had tears in my eyes. I said a couple of words I can't remember.

For the next couple of weeks the phone wouldn't stop ringing. There were all sorts of clubs and schools wanting to hear me speak. I wrote the names and addresses down on pieces of paper and all over the walls of the apartment.

I went totally into speaking out against the war after that. I went into it the same way I'd gone into everything else I've wanted to do in my life—the way I'd gone into pole vaulting or baseball or the marines. But this was something that meant much more than being an athlete or a marine. I could see that this thing—this body I had trained so hard to be strong and quick, this body I now dragged around with me like an empty corpse—was to mean much more than I had ever realized. Much more than I'd known the night I cried into my pillow in Massaqequa because my youth had been desecrated, my physical humanity defiled. I think I honestly believed that if only I could speak out to enough people I could stop the war myself. I honestly believed people would listen to me because of who I was, a wounded American veteran. They would have to listen. Every chance I had to get my broken body on the tube or in front of an audience I went hog wild. Yes, let them get a look at me. Let them be remined of what they'd done when they'd sent my generation off to war. One look would be enough —worth more than a thousand speeches. But if they wanted speeches I could give them speeches too. There was no end to what I had to tell them.

"I'm the example of the war," I would say. "Look at me. Do you want your sons to look like this? Do you want to put on the uniform and come home like me?" Some people could not believe the conditions I told them about in the hospitals. Others could not believe anything at all. After one of the TV shows a cameraman called me a commie traitor to my face. He was pushing me down the studio steps in my chair and I wondered if he was going to drop me. I kept receiving letters from people calling me names and telling me what they would do if I didn't stop aiding the enemy.

The speaking went on and on, and so did the war, and after a while it all began to seem endless. My friends told me I was starting to sound like a broken record. Even Kenny got disgusted with my new role of activist and antiwar veteran and left for New York. I went a little crazy staying alone in the apartment, answering the phone that never stopped ringing and scrawling more names all over the walls. One night I tore the place apart.

I thought of stopping but I was afraid of the loneliness. The speaking had brought back every-

thing—the hospital, Vietnam. Each time I spoke
about an experience it was just like reliving it.
And there were some things I never talked about
—like the corporal from Georgia and the ambush
in the village and the dead children lying on the
ground.

I can't remember one time when I even came
close to telling anyone exactly what had happened over there. Back then it was still deep inside of me and I shared it with no one—not even
the men I had come to know as my brothers.

THE NOON TRAFFIC is moving along Wilshire Boulevard just as if the line of veterans and ordinary citizens picketing Nixon's campaign headquarters were not there. "Join us!" we cry. "Stop the war!" Heavy curtains are drawn over the windows of the campaign headquarters where volunteers are working for the reelection of the president. We have been there for two days and not one of the volunteers has ever looked out. The people in their cars pass us quickly, intent on their steering wheels. Who are these people going to work, going to lunch, as if nothing is more important than that? "Here!" I scream. "Look at the war!" They never so much as turn their heads. I wheel out into the traffic, pushing myself in front of cars. "Take a good look at the war!" I cry, racing with my wheelchair in front of a truck. I do not think—or even care—about getting killed. I am screaming at them to look at me. Up on the rooftop of the headquarters the hidden police cameras are taking pictures, and I know that all by myself I have at least succeeded in stopping traffic.

One by one the other demonstrators are breaking from the line. They sit down among the cars, banging their picket sticks and yelling, their voices hoarse—"One, two, three, four. We don't want your fucking war"—tying up the traffic for blocks. We have taken the streets. People are honking their horns now, workers and secretaries hanging out their windows, busdrivers shouting their approval. Some of the demonstrators are dancing and I grab both wheels of my chair, then let go with one hand and raise my middle finger in the air as a salute to the cops and the FBI. I spin on my two wheels in front of everyone, as the shouting goes on for the war to end, for the killing to be stopped forever. I keep doing my wheelies as the police look on with envy and utter contempt, frozen on their side of the street. They seem torn between wanting to kill us and wanting to tear off their uniforms and throw away their guns. "Come join us!" we shout to them, but they do not take us up on our invitation.

Finally a tall lieutenant announces over a bullhorn that the demonstration has ended and that everyone is to clear out immediately. "How are you doing, brother?" says a man with long red hair in back of me. "Is everything okay?" He is someone I have seen at other demonstrations, but I do not know his name. "You look like you could use some help," he says, and offers to push me for a while.

The police are moving now, closing in on us. I can hear sirens in the distance. I begin yelling and screaming directions to the people around me. "Get back on the sidewalk into the line! Come on now!" I try to wheel my chair forward, but it will not move. I try again.

Suddenly the man with the red hair is leaning over from behind me, grabbing my hands. "You're under arrest." Another man whom I recognize from the picket line runs up to help him. "Come on you bastard. You're going to jail!"

I am fighting to keep them from handcuffing me, screaming for the other demonstrators to help me.

The red-headed man lifts up the handles of my chair and dumps me into the street. I fall forward on my face, my legs twisted under me.

"Get your fucking hands behind you!" The red-headed man jabs his knee into my back.

There is a tremendous commotion all around me. Someone is kicking the dead part of my body that can't feel anymore. People are yelling and screaming and clubs are flying everywhere.

"I'm a Vietnam veteran! Don't you know what you're doing to me? Oh God, what's happening." They are holding my arms. They twist them behind my back, clamp handcuffs around my wrists.

"Don't you understand? My body's paralyzed. I can't move my body, I can't feel my body."

"Get him the fuck out of here!" yells someone.

Kicking me and hitting me with their fists, they begin dragging me along. They tear the medals I have won in the war from my chest and throw me back into the chair, my hands still cuffed behind me. I feel myself falling forward because I cannot balance and the red-headed man keeps pushing me back against the chair, yelling and cursing at me to stay put.

"I have no stomach muscles, don't you understand?"

"Shut up you sonofabitch!"

There are women standing on the sidewalk nearby crying, and all around me people are being beaten and handcuffed. The two men begin dragging me in the chair to an unmarked car on the other side of the street.

The red-headed man throws my body into the back seat, my dead limbs flopping underneath me. "Get in there you fucking traitor!"

I am feeling hurt all over and I can hardly breathe. I lie bleeding in the back seat as a discussion goes on between the two of them about whether or not they have broken any of my bones. I hear them say they are going to take me to the county jail hospital for x-rays.

Something happens to them when I take my clothes off in the admitting room. They stand there looking at me. They see my scars and the rubber catheter tube going into my penis and they begin to think they have made a mistake. I can see the fear in their faces. They have just beaten up a half-dead man, and they know it. They are very careful now, almost polite. They help me put my clothes back on when the doctor is through with me.

"I was in Vietnam too," the red-headed man says, hesitating.

"We don't want the war either," says the other cop. "No one wants war."

They help me back into the chair and take me to another part of the prison building to be booked.

"What's your name?" the officer behind the desk says.

"Ron Kovic," I say. "Occupation, Vietnam veteran against the war."

"What?" he says sarcastically, looking down at me.

"I'm a Vietnam veteran against the war," I almost shout back.

"You should have died over there," he says. He turns to his assistant. "I'd like to take this guy and throw him off the roof."

They fingerprint me and take my picture and put me in a cell. I have begun to wet my pants like a little baby. The tube has slipped out during my examination by the doctor. I try to fall asleep but even though I am exhausted, the anger is alive in me like a huge hot stone in my chest. I lean my head up against the wall and listen to the toilets flush again and again.

They lead me out of the cell the next morning around ten o'clock. I am to be moved to another part of the prison until someone comes to bail me out. They have arrested seventeen other vets at the demonstration. They take them out of the cells one by one, handcuffing and chaining them together in a long line like a chain gang. I look at their faces and wonder which one of them is like the guy with long red hair and the other cop who'd pretended to be veterans the day before. Which one is the informer now? I think to myself.

They tell me to move out of the way. They cannot fit me into the line with the others. "It's too difficult with that chair of yours," one of the cops complains.

"Don't you want to put the cuffs on me again?" I say. "Don't you think I need leg chains like the others?"

He looks at me surprised, then turns away and screams, "Let's go!"

The veterans clank their chains against the cold cement floor as they file past me out of the cellblock. Seventeen of America's veterans dragging those chains, handcuffed together—America's children. I cry because I want to be walking with them and because I want so much to trust them. But after what has happened I don't know whether I will be able to trust anyone, even my closest friends now. What are they doing to me? I think. They have taken so much from me already and still they are not satisfied. What more will they take?

AFTER A SPEECH in a church in Compton I met a woman. I had the whole congregation in tears and a pretty woman in a long dress came up to me afterward and we started talking. We went outside and we kept talking until late that night. She gave me her phone number and told me she had two kids and if I wasn't doing anything the next week to drop by. She was a schoolteacher and her name was Helen. We called each other every day that week and one night I went over to her house. I kissed her in the driveway with the motor still running in my fancy Oldsmobile. It was the first time I had been close to a woman since Mexico. She called me the next day and told me she loved me. I thought it was pretty silly at first.

I went up to the mountains with a group of Quakers soon after that. I remember staying up all night at a house near their training school. It was a house that belonged to this crippled guy— I think he'd had polio. His wife had divorced him, but she was up there that weekend in his house with her boyfriend, making it on the couch. The guy in the wheelchair wasn't there, but even if he had been, they said he wouldn't have minded. I remember they gave me his room to stay in, and there were shelves in it with hundreds of books. I stayed awake all night and when I finally got up the next morning I threw up in the toilet bowl. I was thinking about the guy's wife on the couch with her boyfriend, and about Helen who said she loved me.

I called her up as soon as I got back. It was really nice to have someone love me, I said, and I listened to her tell it to me again. I went over to her house that night and slept with her in her bed. She had this little room that was near the kitchen and she had a photograph in it, a wedding photograph of herself and her ex–old man all dressed up in the finest things. She said he was a drifter but she still cared about him. He just wasn't responsible enough to take care of her and the two kids. I remember she played soft music on the radio. The whole thing gave me a funny empty feeling. I slept with her the second time just before I went back to New York. I told her I was leaving and that I would see her in a month or two. I didn't tell her it bothered me that she was calling me all the time now telling me she loved me. I said I'd had enough of California.

I remember freaking out a couple of times when I got home, crying in front of my mother, telling her about the babies I had killed. I thought

I was losing my mind. The dead corporal from Georgia was finally catching up with me and hanging me in almost all my dreams. Every day I woke up with a pain in my chest. I felt scared and shaky. I broke down one night and called Helen. "I think I want to marry you," I remember saying.

"Are you sure?" I heard her say over and over on the phone. "Are you sure you want to marry me?"

"Yeah," I said. "I love you baby and I want to marry you."

Next thing I knew she was flying across the country with two screaming kids to meet my family.

I met her at the airport. She was wearing red tights and I remember she had cut her hair. I'd really liked her hair long but when I went to the airport her hair was short and the kids looked terrible too. I didn't know how to tell her about her hair.

I remember she wanted to go to church that day to say a few prayers for something or other. I drove her over there but I wouldn't go in. I sat in the car and turned up the radio. A song was playing called "Bye-Bye Miss American Pie" and I remember listening to it and feeling real sad inside, real low like I wanted to cry or kill someone.

She came back into the car and we drove all over the neighborhood. I kept stopping and introducing her to people I knew. "Helen and I are getting married," I said. I even introduced her to Castiglia, who was visiting his folks that weekend, pushing away from him in the wheelchair after I told him I was going to marry her.

By the time we left Massapequa we were fighting about everything all the time and I was getting sick of the whole thing. She was always talking to me about going back to church and meeting married couples and building a strong family for the future. We hadn't even been able to sleep together much. I'd had to stay on the couch on the porch and she was down in Sue's room with the kids. My mother and dad never wanted a man and woman that weren't married sleeping together even if the woman was divorced and had two kids.

We tried living together for a while when we got back to California, first at my house and then at hers. I don't know why I ever did it or why I ever asked her to marry me, but back then it seemed really important to have someone like Helen to hold on to. I even ended up going down to the V.A. hospital in Long Beach and seeing a marriage counselor for paralyzed men. The counselor and I sat out in the sun a lot and fed birds and shouted at each other but it never worked. Every time I came home from the sessions I threw up and finally I couldn't even sleep near Helen anymore. I knew I had to be alone for a while. I found a small house on Hurricane Street in Santa Monica and moved into it.

WHEN I FIRST MOVED to Hurricane Street it was quiet. I wanted to get away not only from Helen but from everything that reminded me of the war. I was going to grow plants and cook my own food. I had a lot of dreams about how it was going to be. I even wanted to write a book. I bought an old rolltop desk and spent an afternoon with a couple of friends going to pick it up and moving it into the house.

It was a beautiful little house a block from the ocean—more a small neat shack tucked into an alleyway. The windows were wooden hurricane slats, which gave the place the appearance of always being ready for a hurricane or a big storm. There was a shower that had been adjusted for me so I could fit the wheelchair in comfortably, and I loved being so close to the ocean. I went out one afternoon and bought a big waterbed, the first one I'd ever had.

I never talked too much to my neighbors, except when I was emptying garbage or something.

I used to sit at the window and stare at a dog that was always on the roof of the house in front of me. After the first couple of days I gave up cooking and started eating out at the Jack-in-the-Box hamburger stands. The food was awful, but it was better to be out in the car than stuck alone in the house all the time.

Sometimes I'd have terrible nightmares about the war. I'd wake up scared in my room in the middle of the night. There was no one to hold on to, just myself there inside my frozen body. I remember watching flowers bloom outside my window and feeling good when the ants would come into the house. Well, at least I've got some company, I thought.

I wrote a poem once at my rolltop desk. It was called "Hurricanes/in the eye of the hurricane." I wrote about the loneliness and the silence of my house, how being there was like a sudden pause in the middle of a wild swirling storm. A lot of times I couldn't take it. I'd get into my car and drive as far and fast as I could. But after a while I learned to stay by myself for a long time.

The time since the war was passing so fast now and he wasn't in the hospital anymore and they weren't smiling down by his bedside and the priests weren't there and he wasn't in the streets speaking out against the men who had made all the terrible things that happened to him possible. They weren't cheering and clapping or even putting the handcuffs on him anymore. He wasn't in jail and in jail at least he knew there were other people around to talk to but now there was no one and all the cheering and all the clapping had stopped and now he was more alone than he had ever been in his life.

What kind of miserable life was this, no friends, no legs, people staring at him wherever he went. The depression sometimes was awesome, like he was drowning in it, and no matter how hard he tried he wasn't ever getting out. He had tried so hard for years to hold on. He had even sometimes invented things that weren't true, made believe so the feelings would go away. But now he wasn't making things up anymore, he was too tired to do that, in too much pain. Where were his legs that used to run? he thought.

. He wanted people around him. He wanted someone to call him on the phone. He wanted just one friend he could talk to about the real things, the painful truths about his miserable existence that would make most people walk away from him—"Sorry I gotta run now. I'm late already." Other people always seemed able to laugh and joke about the whole thing, but they weren't the one who was living in this angry numb corpse, they didn't have to wake up each morning and feel the dead weight of these legs and strain the yellow urine into the ugly rubber bag, they didn't have to put on the rubber gloves each morning over the bathroom bowl and dig into his rear end to clean the brown chunks of shit out. They lived very easy lives, why their lives were disgustingly easy compared to his and they acted sometimes like everything was equal and he was the same as them, but he knew they were lying and especially the women, when they lay with him and told him how much they loved his body, how it wasn't any different than any other man's, that they didn't care if his dick was numb and dead and he couldn't feel warm and good inside a woman ever again. He was a half-dead corpse and no one could tell him any different. They could use the fancy medical words like they had in the hospital but he knew who they had brought back with all their new helicopters and wonderful new ways of killing people, all that incredible advancement in technology. He would never have come back from any other war. But now here he was. He was back and dead and breathing. Oh Mom, oh Dad, somebody, Jesus, somebody please help me. No one to love him, no one to touch him the way he had been touched before the war. He was a little speck now, he was a tiny little dot and he had to do something fast because he felt himself getting smaller and smaller. He had to live again, feel again.

He had been born on the Fourth of July, he had been their Yankee Doodle Dandy, their all-American boy. He had given them almost his whole being in the war and now, after all that, they weren't satisfied with three-quarters being gone, they wanted to take the rest of him. It was crazy but he knew that's what they wanted. They wanted his head and his mind, the numb legs and the wheelchair, they wanted everything. It had all been one big dirty trick and he didn't know what to think anymore. All he had tried to do was tell the truth about the war. But now he just wanted it to be quiet, to be where they weren't cursing at him and beating him and jailing him, lying and calling him a traitor. He had never been anything but a thing to them, a thing to put a uniform on and train to kill, a young thing to run through the meat-grinder, a cheap small nothing thing to make mincemeat out of.

And somewhere along the way he had forgotten to be polite anymore, and how to be a nice person. Somewhere through it all they had taken even that and he wanted it back so much, so very desperately, he would give almost anything to be able to be kind to people again, but the big machine, the one that had given him the number and the rifle, had sucked it out of him forever. They had made him confused and uncertain and blind with hate. They wanted to make him hide like he was hiding now. How many more, he thought, how many more like him were out there hiding on a thousand other Hurricane Streets? He was a living reminder of something terrible and awful. No matter what they said to him, no matter how much they tried to twist and bend things, he held on to what he knew and all the terrible things he had seen and done for them. They had buried the corporal and the children he had killed in the ground, but he was still sitting and breathing in his wheelchair, and now the last thing he could do for them if he wasn't going to die was to disappear.

He knew too much about them. He knew, goddamn it, like no one else would ever know. They were small men with small ideas, gamblers and hustlers who had gambled with his life and hustled him off to the war. They were smooth talkers, men who wore suits and smiled and were polite, men who wore watches and sat behind big desks sticking pins in maps in rooms he had never seen, men who had long-winded telephone conversations and went home to their wives and children. They were like the guy on television who hid the little pea under the three cups, moving them back and forth, back and forth, until you got real confused and didn't know where the hell anything was. They had never seen blood and guts and heads and arms. They had never picked up the shattered legs of children and watched the blood drip into the sand below their feet. It was they who were the little dots, the small cheap things, not him and the others they had sent to do their killing.

He had to rise up out of this deep dark prison. He had to come back. He knew the power he had. Maybe he had forgotten it for a while but it was still there and he could feel it growing in his mind, bigger and bigger—the power to make people remember, to make them as angry as he was every day of his life, every moment of his existence. He would come back very soon and he would make it like all the stories of the baseball players he had read when he was a kid. *"He's picking up the ball. He's running across the field. Kovic is making a terrific comeback, folks! A terrific comeback. . . ."*

6

EVERY ONCE IN a while as I drive the Oldsmobile down the long, hot Texas highway, I look into the dust-covered rearview mirror and see the convoy behind me, stretching back like a gigantic snake so far I cannot even tell where it ends—cars and buses, trucks and jeeps, painted with flowers and peace signs, a strange caravan of young men wearing war ribbons on torn utility jackets and carrying plastic guns. It is August of 1972 and we have come nearly two thousand miles with another thousand still ahead of us before we reach Miami. We have shared food and cans of Coke. We have driven like madmen across the desert and lain down in the sand in our sleeping bags. We have played and laughed around campfires. It is our last patrol together, and I know I will remember it as long as I live. It is a historic event like the Bonus March of thousands of veterans upon the Capitol in the thirties. And now it is we who are marching, the boys of the fifties. We are going to the Republi-

can National Convention to reclaim America and
a bit of ourselves. It is war and we are soldiers
again, as tight as we have ever been, a whole lost
generation of dope-smoking kids in worn jungle
boots coming from all over the country to tell
Nixon a thing or two. We know we are fighting
the real enemies this time—the ones who have
made profit off our very lives. We have lain all
night in the rain in ambush together. We have
burned anthills with kerosene and stalked through
Sally's Woods with plastic machine guns, shooting
people out of trees. We have been a generation
of violence and madness, of dead Indians and
drunken cowboys, of iron pipes full of match-
heads.

There is a tremendous downpour just outisde
of Houston that almost tears the windshield wip-
ers off the car. And after the rain there is one
of the most beautiful rainbows I have ever seen,
and then a second rainbow appears—a magnifi-
cent double rainbow above our heads. I am certain
I want to be alive forever. I know that no matter
what has happened the world is a beautiful place,
and I am here with my brothers.

We drive into Louisiana through the little
towns, past waving schoolchildren and smiling
gas-station attendants flashing the peace sign and
faces looking curiously at us from windows, not
angry just curious and friendly, surprisingly
friendly—the ordinary working people who want
the war to end too, the glory John Wayne war.
But I am scared in Louisiana. Like a lot of the
other guys I think the KKK is all over the place

and someone says there is no difference between the Klan and the cops, they are both the same thing.

He probably hated niggers, the corporal from Georgia. All through the South, these roads, the memories are talking.

He probably hated niggers. Pushing shoving, moving grooving, sliding diving into the coffin, into the soft earth of Georgia. Brought him back in and some guys sent him down the river where all of the dead went to, all the nineteen-year-old corpses who had to be fixed up, shot full of stuff and preserved real good so they could be packaged like meat in the deli to be sent home where their mothers and their sisters and their fathers and their wives could stand and pray and talk about what they were like when they were alive. She'd probably remember better than most of them what it was like to hold his hand, walk with him, kiss him on his soft lips that were now cold and dead, planted six feet in the Georgia mud. Nothing will bring him back, nothing on earth will bring him back. The corporal's dead and he's dead because of me. Oh god, oh Jesus, I want to cry, I want to scream, I want him to be alive again, I want him to be alive again I want him to be alive again oh god oh Jesus oh god o god ogod help me, make him feel, bring him back, bring him back wailing and talking, breathing and laughing again. Who who who who who is he? Now he's finished in the earth, in the ground. Try not to think about it, the thought, the dead thought. Goddamn, goddamn, goddamn fuckin' southern bigot. They were all that way in boot camp. Yes yes I remember. I want school and sitting on the fence and where's Mom and the heater, Richie and me stringing high-tension stickballs, eggballs, baseballs, r r r r r r r run the bases to Castiglia's basement. I want out, I want out, I want out mom mom mom mom mom mom. Take a drag of the cigarette Yes thank you. Can't move, can't you see Richie, can't move, no more posters, teacher's dirty looks, no more warm good red checkered table . . . let me out let me out.

And the Last Patrol moved into the silence and darkness of Louisiana, the long snake, long line of us packed together, moving slower and slower, following the cops under the swaying beautiful trees, the warm muggy night, so warm and muggy and nice and getting ready to rain. Okay okay everybody! Someone screaming into a bullhorn and we are easing into the campsite, circling around like Gabby Hayes and the wagon trains, like a big 360 in the Nam. People crawling into their sleeping bags all over the tall swampy grass, crawling in and pulling them up over their heads dreaming of illumination canisters, or popping red flares in the DMZ, they make love like morphine, rolling and driving together like tomorrow will never come. *What gave them the right to beat me, the war, the scar, the scar in the chair, in the road, for whose trophy case this time Mr. President?*

There is a bridge that goes into Miami and we moved over it like a returning army, like a returning army we moved together slowly across the bridge, our horns blasting, our flags waving, shouting into the wind that blew from the ocean. Once we crossed the bridge we headed through the city, headlights burning on all the cars and trucks. A quick decision was made and we went through every red light and stop sign in the town. I remember hanging out of the Oldsmobile with the big upside-down flag flapping, screaming and shouting as we came nearer and nearer to Flamingo Park. This was the end of the journey and as we approached the park we were beseiged by hundreds and hundreds of well-wishers yelling and cheering and clapping the arrival of the veterans. People were dancing in the streets, playing flutes, running up to us, Yippies and Zippies shoving handfuls of joints into our laps and all the brothers were climbing out of their cars hugging and jumping on top of each other, singing and screaming and carrying on like we had just won the war.

A couple of vets from New York who knew me ran up and hugged me, welcoming me to the enormous tent city. "Yeah man," one of them said, "I read about you in New York when they beat you up. Good to see you down here, good to have you down." I found a place to put my rubber mattress and plant my upside-down American flag. I sat down and looked at all the wild activity around me. Later in the afternoon one of the first reporters came by. "I've got a few things to say," I told her, and we talked for about two hours until she had to go. It got dark and all of us went to sleep. The Yippies and the Zippies were still smoking dope and carrying on in a wild pot party but the Last Patrol was tired. It had been a long journey across America.

It WAS THE night of Nixon's acceptance speech and now I was on my own deep in his territory, all alone in my wheelchair in a sweat-soaked marine utility jacket covered with medals from the war. A TV producer I knew from the Coast had gotten me past the guards at the entrance with his press pass. My eyes were still smarting from teargas. Outside the chain metal fence around the Convention Center my friends were being clubbed and arrested, herded into wagons. The crowds were thick all around me, people dressed as if they were going to a banquet, men in expensive summer suits and women in light elegant dresses. Every once in a while someone would look at me as if I didn't belong there. But I had come almost three thousand miles for this meeting with the president and nothing was going to prevent it from taking place.

I worked my way slowly and carefully into the huge hall, moving down one of the side aisles. "Excuse me, excuse me," I said to delegates as I pushed past them farther and farther to the front of the hall toward the speakers' podium.

I had gotten only halfway toward where I wanted to be when I was stopped by one of the convention security marshals. "Where are you going?" he said. He grabbed hold of the back of my chair. I made believe I hadn't heard him and kept turning my wheels, but his grip on the chair was too tight and now two other security men had joined him.

"What's the matter?" I said. "Can't a disabled veteran who fought for his country sit up front?"

The three men looked at each other for a moment and one of them said, "I'm afraid not. You're not allowed up front with the delegates." I had gotten as far as I had on sheer bluff alone and now they were telling me I could go no farther. "You'll have to go to the back of the convention hall, son. Let's go," said the guard who was holding my chair.

In a move of desperation I swung around facing all three of them, shouting as loud as I could so Walter Cronkite and the CBS camera crew that was just above me could hear me and maybe even focus their cameras in for the six o'clock news. "I'm a Vietnam veteran and I fought in the war! Did you fight in the war?"

One of the guards looked away.

"Yeah, that's what I thought," I said. "I bet none of you fought in the war and you guys are trying to throw me out of the convention. I've got just as much right to be up front here as any of these delegates. I fought for that right and I was born on the Fourth of July."

I was really shouting now and another officer came over. I think he might have been in charge of the hall. He told me I could stay where I was if I was quiet and didn't move up any farther. I agreed with the compromise. I locked my brakes and looked for other veterans in the tremendous crowd. As far as I could tell, I was the only one who had made it in.

People had begun to sit down all around me. They all had Four More Years buttons and I was surprised to see how many of them were young. I began speaking to them, telling them about the Last Patrol and why veterans from all over the United States had taken the time and effort to travel thousands of miles to the Republican National Convention. "I'm a disabled veteran!" I shouted. "I served two tours of duty in Vietnam and while on my second tour of duty up in the DMZ I was wounded and paralyzed from the chest down." I told them I would be that way for the rest of my life. Then I began to talk about the hospitals and how they treated the returning veterans like animals, how I, many nights in the Bronx, had lain in my own shit for hours waiting for an aide. "And they never come," I said. "They never come because that man that's going to accept the nomination tonight has been lying to all of us and spending the money on war that should be spent on healing and helping the wounded. That's the biggest lie and hypocrisy of all—that we had to go over there and fight and get crippled and come home to a government and leaders who could care less about the same boys they sent over."

I kept shouting and speaking, looking for some kind of reaction from the crowd. No one seemed to want to even look at me.

"Is it too real for you to look at? Is this wheel-chair too much for you to take? The man who will accept the nomination tonight is a liar!" I shouted again and again, until finally one of the security men came back and told me to be quiet or they would have to take me to the back of the hall.

I told him that if they tried to move me or touch my chair there would be a fight and hell to pay right there in front of Walter Cronkite and the national television networks. I told him if he wanted to wrestle me and beat me to the floor of the convention hall in front of all those cameras he could.

By then a couple of newsmen, including Roger Mudd from CBS, had worked their way through the security barricades and begun to ask me questions.

"Why are you here tonight?" Roger Mudd asked me. "But don't start talking until I get the camera here," he shouted.

It was too good to be true. In a few seconds Roger Mudd and I would be going on live all over the country. I would be doing what I had come here for, showing the whole nation what the war was all about. The camera began to roll, and I began to explain why I and the others had come, that the war was wrong and it had to stop immediately. "I'm a Vietnam veteran," I said. "I gave America my all and the leaders of this government threw me and the others away to rot in their V.A. hospitals. What's happening in Vietnam is a crime against humanity, and I just want the American people to know that we have come all the way across this country, sleeping on the ground and in the rain, to let the American people see for themselves the men who fought their war and have come to oppose it. If you can't believe the veteran who fought the war and was wounded in the war, who can you believe?"

"Thank you," said Roger Mudd, visibly moved by what I had said. "This is Roger Mudd," he said, "down on the convention floor with Ron Kovic, a disabled veteran protesting President Nixon's policy in Vietnam."

The security agents were frantically trying to stop other cameras from getting through and later I was to learn that Press Secretary Ronald Ziegler had almost flipped out when he heard Mudd had interviewed me and it had gone nationwide for almost two minutes.

By this time a few other veterans had managed to get into the hall. One of them came to tell me that my old friend Bobby Muller and Bill Wieman, a double amputee, had gotten passes from Congressman McCloskey and had managed to get into the center aisle in direct line with the podium almost two hundred feet back. "Get me up there quick," I said. He turned me around and wheeled me toward the back past the smiling security officers who must have thought I was leaving. What are you smiling at? I thought to myself. I'm just warming up.

"There, up there," the vet said, pointing to the front of the aisle where Bobby and Bill were sitting in their wheelchairs.

"Where you been?" Wieman said to me, as I shook their hands.

"I've been over there," I said, pointing to the other aisle. "I wanted to get all the way to the front, but this place is great."

We lined ourselves up together, wheelchair to wheelchair, facing the platform where Nixon would speak. They had brought in a couple of Stop the War signs, and I grabbed one and held it above my head.

There was an announcement at the podium and then a tremendous roar. It was the vice president of the United States, Spiro T. Agnew. The delegates stood chanting and shaking their clasped hands over their heads, stamping their feet up and down until it seemed as though the whole convention hall was going to explode. "Four more years," the crowd shouted. "Four more years, four more years."

Agnew stood rigid at attention, accepting the tumultuous applause. Finally he raised both of his palms, signaling them all to stop so he could give his speech. Every time he spoke a few words, he was interrupted by the wild crowd, wild and enthusiastic. "Agnew in 'seventy-six!" a fat woman yelled next to me. "Agnew in 'seventy-six!"

I pulled myself up onto the siderail of my wheel-

chair and sat holding my sign as high as I could.
I wanted everyone in the hall to be able to see it.
A man came up suddenly from my blind side.
Before I knew what hit me he had grabbed my
sign and torn it into shreds in front of me. "You
lousy commie sonofabitch!" he shouted.

Now there was only one sign left and we decided to hold on to it until it was Nixon's turn to
speak. A few seconds before he was introduced,
security agents began to move in all around us.
We must have been an ugly sight to the National
Republican Party as we sat there in perfect view
of all the national networks that were perched
above us.

Suddenly a roar went up in the convention
hall, louder than anything I had ever heard in
my life. It started off as a rumble, then gained in
intensity until it sounded like a tremendous
thunderbolt. "Four more years, four more years,"
the crowd roared over and over again. The fat
woman next to me was jumping up and down and
dancing in the aisle. It was the greatest ovation
the president of the United States had ever received and he loved it. I held the sides of my
wheelchair to keep my hands from shaking. After
what seemed forever, the roar finally began to die
down.

This was the moment I had come three thousand miles for, this was it, all the pain and the
rage, all the trials and the death of the war and
what had been done to me and a generation of
Americans by all the men who had lied to us and
tricked us, by the man who stood before us in the

convention hall that night, while men who had fought for their country were being gassed and beaten in the street outside the hall. I thought of Bobby who sat next to me and the months we had spent in the hospital in the Bronx. It was all hitting me at once, all those years, all that destruction, all that sorrow.

President Nixon began to speak and all three of us took a deep breath and shouted at the top of our lungs, "Stop the bombing, stop the war, stop the bombing, stop the war," as loud and as hard as we could, looking directly at Nixon. The security agents immediately threw up their arms, trying to hide us from the cameras and the president. "Stop the bombing, stop the bombing," I screamed. For an instant Cronkite looked down, then turned his head away. They're not going to show it, I thought. They're going to try and hide us like they did in the hospitals. Hundreds of people around us began to clap and shout "Four more years," trying to drown out our protest. They all seemed very angry and shouted at us to stop. We continued shouting, interrupting Nixon again and again until Secret Service agents grabbed our chairs from behind and began pulling us backward as fast as they could out of the convention hall. "Take it easy," Bobby sad to me. "Don't fight back."

I wanted to take a swing and fight right there in the middle of the convention hall in front of the president and the whole country. "So this is how they treat their wounded veterans!" I screamed.

A short guy with a big Four More Years button ran up to me and spat in my face. "Traitor!" he screamed, as he was yanked back by police. Pandemonium was breaking out all around us and the Secret Service men kept pulling us out backward.

"I served two tours of duty in Vietnam!" I screamed to one newsman. "I gave three-quarters of my body for America. And what do I get? Spit in the face!" I kept screaming until we hit the side entrance where the agents pushed us outside and shut the doors, locking them with chains and padlocks so reporters wouldn't be able to follow us out for interviews.

All three of us sat holding on to each other shaking. We had done it. It had been the biggest moment of our lives, we had shouted down the president of the United States and disrupted his acceptance speech. What more was there left to do but go home?

I sat in my chair still shaking and began to cry.

7

ALL HIS LIFE he'd wanted to be a winner. It was always so important to win, to be the very best. He thought back to high school and the wrestling team and out on Lee Place and Hamilton Avenue when he and the rest of the boys had played stickball or football. He thought back to that and remembered how hard he'd tried to win even in those simple games.

But now it all seemed different. All the hopes about being the best marine, winning all those medals. They all seemed crushed now, they were gone forever. Like the man he had just killed with one shot, all these things had disappeared and he knew, he was very certain, they would never come back again. It had been so simple when he was back on the block with Richie or running down to the deli to pick up a pack of Topps baseball cards, even working in the food store that summer before he went to the war now seemed like a real nice thing. It seemed like so much nicer a thing than what was happening around him now, all the faces, the torn green fatigues, and just below his foot was the guy's head with a gaping hole through his throat.

The Amtrac was heading back to the thick barbed wire where the battalion lived and everyone around him was quiet. There was no question in his mind they all knew what had happened— that he had just pulled the little metal trigger and put a slug through the corporal's neck.

Inside he felt everything sort of squeezing in on him. His hands kept rubbing up and down his leg. He was very nervous and his finger, the one that pulled the trigger, was sort of scratching his leg now.

Later, when they got back to the battalion area, he gave a quick report to a young lieutenant in the major's bunker. "They were attacking," he said, looking at the lieutenant's face, "and we moved backward."

"You retreated," the lieutenant said.

"Yes, we retreated and he got shot. He lived a little while but then he died. He died there in the sand and we called for help. And then we put him in the Amtrac. He must have run away when they started firing. It was dark and I couldn't tell."

"Okay," said the young-looking lieutenant. "Come back again in the morning and we can go over it again. Too bad about . . ." he said.

"Yeah," he said.

He was almost crying now as he turned and walked out of the big command bunker. There

was sand all over the place outside and a cold
monsoon wind was blowing. He looked out into
the darkness and heard the waves of the China
Sea breaking softly far away.

There was a path made of wooden ammo casings that led back to his tent. He walked on it
like a man on a tightrope, it was so dark and so
very hard to see. A couple of times he stumbled
on the wooden boxes. It was quiet as he opened
the tent flap, as quiet and dark as it had been outside the major's bunker. He dragged in carrying
his rifle in one hand and the map case in the
other. They were all asleep, all curled up on their
cots, inside their mosquito nets. He walked up to
his rack and sat down, his head sinking down to
the floor. Panic was still rushing through him like
a wild train, his heart still raced through his chest
as he saw over and over again the kid from
Georgia running toward him and the crack of his
rifle killing him dead.

I killed him, he kept repeating over and over
to himself.

He's dead, he thought.

Gripping his rifle, holding the trigger, he went
through the whole thing again and again, tapping,
touching the trigger lightly each time he saw the
corporal from Georgia running toward him just
as he had out there in the sand when everything
seemed so crazy and frightening. Each time he
felt his heart racing as the three cracks went off
and the dark figure slumped to the sand in front
of him.

"He's dead—go get him!" someone was yelling

to his right. "Go get him he's hit!" Someone was running now, running to the body and they were pulling the guy in. They were bringing him back to the trench where they all lay scared and shivering.

"Doc—Doc—where's the corpsman!" somebody was yelling.

"Hey Doc, hurry up!" Then somebody said it. Somebody shouted real loud, "It's corporal. They got corporal . . ."

"He's dead," somebody said. "He's gone."

Slowly he turned the rifle around and pointed the barrel toward his head. Oh Jesus God almighty, he thought. *Why?* Why? Why? He began to cry slowly at first. *Why?* I'm going to kill myself, he thought. I'm going to pull this trigger. He was going mad. One minute he wanted to pull the trigger and the next he was feeling the strange power of a man who had just killed someone.

He laid the weapon down by the side of his rack and crawled in with his clothing still on. I killed him, he kept thinking, and when I wake up tomorrow, he thought, when I wake up tomorrow it will still be the same. He wanted to run and hide. He felt like he was in boot camp again and there was no escape, no way off the island. He would wake up with the rest of them the next day. He would get up and wash outside the tent in his tin dish, he would shave and go to chow. But everything would not be all right, he thought, nothing would be all right at all. It was starting to be very different now, very different from what he had ever thought possible.

He opened his eyes slowly as the light came
into the tent like a bright triangle. They were all
starting to stir, the other men, starting to get up.
And then he remembered again what had happened. He hadn't killed any Communist, he
thought, he hadn't killed any Communist. Panic
swept through his body. In some wild and crazy
moment the night before he had pulled the trigger and killed one of his own people.

He tried to slow everything down. He had to
think of it as an accident. A lot of guys were
firing their guns, there was so much noise and
confusion going on. And maybe, he tried real hard
to think, maybe he didn't kill the corporal at all,
maybe it was someone else. Didn't everyone else
start firing after his first three shots? Didn't they
all start screaming and shooting after that? Yes,
he thought, that's exactly what happened. They
were all firing too, he thought. I wasn't the
only one. It could have been any of them. Any of
them could have put the slug through the corporal's neck. Maybe it was the Communists who
killed him. Maybe. But that was awfully hard to
believe, that was even harder now to believe than
the other men shooting the corporal. Something
had gone wrong, something crazy had happened
out there and he didn't want to think about it.
He was getting tired of turning it over in his
mind, over and over again. He was getting real
tired of the whole thing. It was all playing so fast
and so hard. It all hurt too much. It wasn't right.
It wasn't fair. He wanted to forget it, but it
wouldn't stop.

He went back to the big sandbagged bunker to see the major.

"That was a pretty rough night, sergeant," the major said, looking up from the green plastic maps on his desk.

"Yes sir," he said. "It was pretty bad."

"Ran into a lot of them, didn't you?" the major said, almost smiling.

"Yes, we sure did. I mean they just sort of popped up on us and started firing."

The major looked down at the maps again and frowned slightly. "What happened?" he said. "What happened out there?"

"Well, major, like I said, we were moving toward the village and we had just grabbed the woman."

"The woman?" the major said.

"Yes, we had just grabbed the pregnant woman."

"She was pregnant?"

"Well yes sir, but we didn't find out until later. We didn't even think she was a woman. She didn't have any chest major, she was flat like a board and we tied her hands behind her back. And there was a boy with her, maybe her small son. We tied his hands too."

"And then?" said the major.

"And then," he said, "we took them up on top of a big sand dune that was a few hundred yards from the village."

"Didn't anybody see you?"

"Yeah," he said. He could feel himself sort of relaxing now. "I think a couple of people in the village. They were going to get water or something. They saw us and one of them started running back to the village. The others just made believe they hadn't seen us at all. I knew they had but they made believe and kept walking back to the village. We set up a perimeter on top of the hill. We set it up so we could watch all around us and see if anyone was coming out of the village after the woman."

"What time was this?" said the major.

"Well—" he looked carefully at his watch. "I think it was about four. It was starting to get dark and I told all the men to eat their rations. Then it became very dark and there were a few small lights in the village and then the shooting started to the left. It was maybe a hundred meters from the big sand dune and I ran to the woman and the kid. I knew she was a woman now and pregnant. Then men started running toward the ocean, away from the dune. Some of them were very frightened. I kept yelling for them to stay, but everyone sort of scattered. Then they all seemed to be running in a line toward a long trench near the ocean. Most of them got back."

"Most of them?" said the major.

"Yeah," he said, "they all got back in the trench except one."

"Who was that?"

"That was corporal, he was the last to come back. And that was when it happened," he said.

"What happened?" said the major.

"That was when the corporal was killed."

The bald sergeant who worked for the major

walked in just as he told the major the thing that had been rolling around in his head all night.

"What happened?" said the major.

The bald sergeant was putting some papers on the major's desk. He did that and walked out.

"There were a bunch of shots," he said carefully. "Everybody was shooting, it was a bad firefight." He paused. "It was pretty bad and then corporal was shot. He was shot and he fell down in front of us and a couple of the men ran out to get him. They pulled him back in. I think the others were still firing. The corpsman tried to help . . . the corporal was shot in the neck . . . The corpsman tried to help . . ."

It was becoming very difficult for him to talk now. "Major," he said, "I think I might have . . . I think I might have killed the corporal."

"I don't think so," said the major quickly.

"It was very confusing. It was hard to tell what was happening."

"Yes I know," said the major. "Sometimes it gets very hard out there. I was out a couple of weeks ago and sometimes it's very hard to tell what's happening."

He stared down at the floor of the bunker until he could make himself say it again. He wasn't quite sure the major had heard him the first time.

"But I just want you to know, major, I think I was the one who killed him. I think it might have been me."

There, he had said it. And now he was walking away.

For some reason he was feeling a lot better.

He had told the major everything and the major hadn't believed it. It was like going to confession when he was a kid and the priest saying everything was okay. He walked by the men outside the radio shack. They turned their faces away as he passed. Let them talk, he thought. He was only human, he had made a mistake. The corporal was dead now and no one could bring him back.

The chaplain held a memorial service that afternoon for the man he had killed and he sat in the tent with the rest of the men. There was a wife and a kid, someone said. He tried to listen to the words the chaplain was saying, the name he kept repeating over and over again. Who was this man he'd just killed? Who had he been? He wanted to scream right there in the church tent, right there during the ceremony. He kept hearing the name too many times, the name of the dead man, the man with the friends, the man with the wife, the one he didn't know or care to know, the kid from Georgia who was now being carefully wrapped up in some plastic bag and sent back in a cheap wooden box to be buried in the earth at nineteen.

He had panicked with the rest of them that night and murdered his first man, but it wasn't the enemy, it wasn't the one they had all been taught and trained to kill, it wasn't the silhouette at the rifle range he had pumped holes in from five hundred yards, or the German soldiers with plastic machine guns in Sally's Woods. He'd never figured it would ever happen this way. It never

did in the movies. There were always the good
guys and the bad guys, the cowboys and the
Indians. There was always the enemy and the
good guys and each of them killed the other.

He went back to his tent after the ceremony
was over and sat down. There was some mail but
he couldn't get interested in it. Someone had sent
him a Sergeant Rock comicbook. But it wasn't
funny anymore. The good guys weren't supposed
to kill the good guys.

The next few weeks passed in a slow way,
much slower than any time in his whole life.
Each day dragged by until the night, the soft
soothing night, when he could close himself off
from the pain, when he could forget the terrible
thing for a few hours. Each night before he slept
he prayed to his god, begging for some understanding of why the thing had happened, why he
had been made into a murderer with one shot.
Why him? he thought over and over again. He
first pleaded with God, then he became angry,
demanding. Oh God, he thought, why did this
happen, for what reason? What kind of god, he
thought, would do this to him? What kind of god
would give him these terrible feelings and nightmares for what seemed to be the rest of his life?

The time passed in big gaps of deadness. Nights
when he could sleep and forget and mornings
when it all came back and the men stood by the
tents looking at him in their peculiar way, whis-
pering on the chow line. He found himself reading
a small pocket Bible so he would not have to look

at them and writing long letters to his mother and
father. He wrote in his diary that he wanted to
become a priest, and that was what he told his
parents in the letter about the corporal that he
finally wrote home. He told them the story he had
told the major, the story about the firefight. And
the whole thing in the letter took on a new and
beautiful meaning. He had seen a man killed and
something, something very deep and wonderful,
had happened to him. In some wonderful way, he
wrote to them, he had become something very
different than he had ever been before. And now,
he told them, he wanted to be a priest. He wanted
to be like the guy up on the altar, the healer and
the guy who gave communion.

He finished the letter and he sent it. There, he
thought, it's through. And now deep down inside
him he still felt the angry pain, but it became a
little easier to live now, easier to live—even
though the war was going on a little worse than
before, artillery and rockets were hitting the camp
almost every day, sending the men into the little
bunkers they had built. The major was still sitting
behind his desk in the big sandbagged battalion
bunker, and whenever he walked past him the
major would return his sharp salute with a very
confident smile on his face. He thought of the
major as his friend. He had understood the whole
terrible thing. He had said that maybe it didn't
happen, things got confusing out there, and the
major said he knew, that he had been out there
himself under heavy fire and he knew.

He knew the major understood everything, like the men who whispered softly on the chow line and the men who stood talking by their tents. No one wants to say, he thought, no one wants to talk about it. Who wanted to approach him and ask if he had done it, if he had killed the corporal that night? No one. No one would ever do it, he thought.

There was a night not long after he had killed the corporal when he was walking on the wooden path that snaked around all the tents past the bunkers like a sidewalk. He was sort of tiptoeing along the casings and he opened up what seemed to be his tent. He had seen this light in the long crack at the bottom of it and he walked in to find he had just walked into the battalion commander's tent. It was very dark, so dark somebody, anybody, could get lost in a place like that, he thought. Just like that goddamn patrol a few months ago when he had read the map wrong, when he had led the men in the wrong direction. He had been a thousand meters off. He was a mile from where he was supposed to be, and now he was doing it again. He was walking in on the goddamn battalion commander who was in his pajamas getting ready to go to bed or something.

"Yes, what do you want, sergeant?" he heard the battalion commander saying to him.

"Ahhh, nothing," he said. "I made a mistake, sir. I thought this was my tent."

The battalion commander looked at him for a

moment, looked at him like he had done a very stupid thing. "Well, carry on," he said.

It was his friend the major who gave him his second chance. He called him into the command bunker one day and told him he wanted him to become the leader of his new scout team. The major who understood him told him he liked the way he operated and said he knew the sergeant could do a good job.

Here was his chance, he thought, to make everything good again. This young, strong marine was getting a second crack at becoming a hero. He knew, he understood, the thing the major was doing for him, and he left the tent feeling stronger and better than he'd felt for a long time. Here was his chance, he thought over and over again.

He walked down the twisting ammo-box side-walk and saluted one of the officers as smartly as ever, much too smartly for anyone who had been over there as long as him. The thoughts of the night he'd killed the corporal were already becoming faded as he began to think more and more about the scout team, how he would train them and the things they would do to make up for all the things that had come before.

He wrote in his diary that night how proud he was to have been made the leader of the scouts, to be serving America in this its most critical hour, just like President Kennedy had talked about. He might get killed, he wrote, but so had a lot of Americans who had fought for democracy. It was very important to be there putting his life on the line, to be going out on patrol and lying in the rain for Sparky the barber and God and the rest. He was proud. He was real proud of what he was doing. This, he thought, is what serving your country is supposed to be about.

HE WENT OUT on patrol with the others the night of the ambush at exactly eight o'clock, loading a round into the chamber of his weapon before he walked outside the tent and into the dark and rain. As usual he had made all the men put on camouflage from head to toe, made sure they had all blackened their faces, and attached twigs and branches to their arms and legs with rubber bands.

One by one the scouts moved slowly past the thick barbed wire and began to walk along the bank of the river, heading toward the graveyard where the ambush would be set up. They were moving north exactly as planned, a line of shadows tightly bunched in the rain. Sometimes it would stop raining and they would spread out somewhat more, but mostly they continued to bunch up together, as if they were afraid of losing their way.

There was a rice paddy on the edge of the graveyard. No one said a word as they walked through it and he thought he could hear voices from the village. He could smell the familiar smoke from the fires in the huts and he knew that the people who went out fishing each day must have come home. They were the people he watched every morning moving quietly in their small boats down toward the mouth of the river, heading out to the sea. Some of the older men reminded him of his father, going to work each morning and coming back home every night to sit by their fires with their children cooking their fish. They must talk about us sometimes, he thought. He wondered a lot what it was they thought about him and the men.

He remembered how difficult it had been when he had first come to the war to tell the villagers from the enemy and sometimes it had seemed easier to hate all of them, but he had always tried very hard not to. He wished he could be sure they understood that he and the men were there because they were trying to help all of them save their country from the Communists.

They were on a rice dike that bordered the graveyard. The voices from the huts nearby seemed quite loud. He looked up ahead to where the lieutenant who had come along with them that night was standing. The lieutenant had sent one of the men, Molina, on across the rice dikes almost to the edge of the village. The cold rain was still coming down very hard and the men behind him were standing like a line of statues waiting for the next command.

But now something was wrong up ahead. He

could see Molina waving his hands excitedly trying to tell the lieutenant something. Stumbling over the dikes, almost crawling, Molina came back toward the lieutenant. He saw him whisper someting in his ear. And now the lieutenant turned and looked at him. "Sergeant," he said, "Molina and I are going to get a look up ahead. Stay here with the team."

Balancing on the dike, he turned slowly after the lieutenant had gone, motioning with his rifle for all of the men in back of him to get down. Each one, carefully, one after the other, squatted along the dike on one knee, waiting in the rain to move out again. They were all shivering from the cold.

They waited for what seemed a long time and then the lieutenant and Molina appeared suddenly through the darkness. He could tell from their faces that they had seen something. They had seen something up ahead, he was sure, and they were going to tell him what they had just seen. He stood up, too excited to stay kneeling down on the dike.

"What is it?" he cried.

"Be quiet," whispered the lieutenant sharply, grabbing his arm, almost throwing him into the paddy. He began talking very quickly and much louder than he should have. "I think we found them. I think we found them," he repeated, almost shouting.

He didn't know what the lieutenant meant. "What?" he said.

"The sappers, the sappers! Let's go!" The lieutenant was taking over now. He seemed very sure of himself, he was acting very confident. "Let's go, goddamn it!"

He clicked his rifle off safety and got his men up quickly, urging them forward, following the lieutenant and Molina toward the edge of the village. They ran through the paddy, splashing like a family of ducks. This time he hoped and prayed it would be the real enemy. He would be ready for them this time. Here was another chance, he thought. He was so excited he ran straight into the lieutenant, bouncing clumsily off his chest.

"I'm sorry, sir," he said.

"Quiet! They're out there," the lieutenant whispered to him, motioning to the rest of the men to get down on their hands and knees now. They crawled to the tree line, then along the back of the rice paddy through almost a foot of water, until the whole team lay in a long line pressed up against the dike, facing the village.

He saw a light, a fire he thought, flickering in the distance off to the right of the village, with little dark figures that seemed to be moving behind it. He could not tell how far away they were from there. It was very hard to tell distance in the dark.

The lieutenant moved next to him. "You see?" he whispered. "Look," he said, very keyed up now. "They've got rifles. Can you see the rifles? Can you see them?" the lieutenant asked him.

He looked very hard through the rain.

"Can you see them?"

"Yes, I see them. I see them," he said. He was very sure.

The lieutenant put his arm around him and whispered in his ear. "Tell them down at the end to give me an illumination. I want this whole place lit up like a fucking Christmas tree."

Turning quickly to the man on his right, he told him what the lieutenant had said. He told him to pass the instructions all the way to the end of the line, where a flare would be fired just above the small fire near the village.

Lying there in the mud behind the dike, he stared at the fire that still flickered in the rain. He could still see the little figures moving back and forth against it like small shadows on a screen. He felt the whole line tense, then heard the WOOOORSHH of the flare cracking overhead in a tremendous ball of sputtering light turning night into day, arching over their heads toward the small fire that he now saw was burning inside an open hut.

Suddenly someone was firing from the end with his rifle, and now the whole line opened up, roaring their weapons like thunder, pulling their triggers again and again without even thinking, emptying everything they had into the hut in a tremendous stream of bright orange tracers that crisscrossed each other in the night.

The flare arched its last sputtering bits into the village and it became dark, and all he could see were the bright orange embers from the fire that had gone out.

And he could hear them.

There were voices screaming.

"What happened? Goddamn it, what happened?" yelled the lieutenant.

The voices were screaming from inside the hut.

"Who gave the order to fire? I wanna know who gave the order to fire."

The lieutenant was standing up now, looking up and down the line of men still lying in the rain.

He found that he was shaking. It had all happened so quickly.

"We better get a killer team out there," he heard Molina say.

"All right, all right. Sergeant," the lieutenant said to him, "get out there with Molina and tell me how many we got."

He got to his feet and quickly got five of the men together, leading them over the dike and through the water to the hut from where the screams were still coming. It was much closer than he had first thought. Now he could see very clearly the smoldering embers of the fire that had been blown out by the terrific blast of their rifles.

Molina turned the beam of his flashlight into the hut. "Oh God," he said. "Oh Jesus Christ." He started to cry. "We just shot up a bunch of kids!"

The floor of the small hut was covered with them, screaming and thrashing their arms back and forth, lying in pools of blood, crying wildly, screaming again and again. They were shot in the face, in the chest, in the legs, moaning and crying.

"Oh Jesus!" he cried.

He could hear the lieutenant shouting at them, wanting to know how many they had killed.

There was an old man in the corner with his head blown off from his eyes up, his brains hanging out of his head like jelly. He kept looking at the strange sight, he had never seen anything like it before. A small boy next to the old man was still alive, although he had been shot many times. He was crying softly, lying in a large pool of blood. His small foot had been shot almost completely off and seemed to be hanging by a thread.

"What's happening? What's going on up there?" The lieutenant was getting very impatient now.

Molina shouted for the lieutenant to come quickly. "You better get up here. There's a lot of wounded people up here."

He heard a small girl moaning now. She was shot through the stomach and bleeding out of the rear end. All he could see now was blood everywhere and he heard their screams with his heart racing like it had never raced before. He felt crazy and weak as he stood there staring at them with the rest of the men, staring down onto the floor like it was a nightmare, like it was some kind of dream and it really wasn't happening.

And then he could no longer stand watching. They were people, he thought, children and old men, people, people like himself, and he had to do something, he had to move, he had to help, do something. He jerked the green medical bag off his back, ripping it open and grabbing for bandages, yelling at Molina to please come and help him. He knelt down in the middle of the screaming bodies and began bandaging them, trying to cover the holes where the blood was still spurting out. "It's gonna be okay. It's gonna be okay," he tried to say, but he was crying now, crying and still trying to bandage them all up. He moved from body to body searching in the dark with his fingers for the holes the bullets had made, bandaging each one as quickly as he could, his shaking hands wet with the blood. It was raining into the hut and a cold wind swept his face as he moved in the dark.

The lieutenant had just come up with the others.

"Help me!" he screamed. "Somebody help!"

"Well, goddamn it sergeant! What's the matter? How many did we kill?"

"They're children!" he screamed at the lieutenant.

"Children and old men!" cried Molina.

"Where are their rifles?" the lieutenant asked.

"There aren't any rifles," he said.

"Well, help him then!" screamed the lieutenant to the rest of the men. The men stood in the entrance of the hut, but they would not move. "Help him, help him. I'm ordering you to help him!"

The men were not moving and some of them were crying now, dropping their rifles and sitting down on the wet ground. They were weeping now with their hands against their faces. "Oh Jesus, oh God, forgive us."

"Forgive us for what we've done!" he heard Molina cry.

"Get up," screamed the lieutenant. "What do you think this is? I'm ordering you all to get up."

Some of the men began slowly crawling over the bodies, grabbing for the bandages that were still left.

By now some of the villagers had gathered outside the hut. He could hear them shouting angrily. He knew they must be cursing them.

"You better get a fucking chopper in here," someone was yelling.

"Where's the radio man? Get the radio man!"

"Hello Cactus Red. This is Red Light Two. Ahhh this is Red Light Two. We need an emergency evac. We got a lot of wounded . . . ahh . . . friendly wounded. A lot of friendly wounded out here." He could hear the lieutenant on the radio, trying to tell the helicopters where to come.

The men in the hut were just sitting there crying. They could not move, and they did not listen to the lieutenant's orders. They just sat with the rain pouring down on them through the roof, crying and not moving.

"You men! You men have got to start listening to me. You gotta stop crying like babies and start acting like marines!" The lieutenant who was off the radio now was shoving the men, pleading with them to move. "You're men, not babies. It's a mistake. It wasn't your fault. They got in the way. Don't you people understand—they got in the goddamn way!"

When the medivac chopper came, he picked up the little boy who was lying next to the old man. His foot came off and he grabbed it up quickly and bandaged it against the bottom stump of the boy's leg. He held him looking into his frightened eyes and carried him up to the open door of the helicopter. The boy was still crying softly when he handed him to the gunner.

And when it was all over and all the wounded had been loaded aboard, he helped the lieutenant move the men back on patrol. They walked away from the hut in the rain. And now he felt his body go numb and heavy, feeling awful and sick inside like the night the corporal had died, as they moved along in the dark and the rain behind the lieutenant toward the graveyard.

It WAS GETTING very cold and it was raining almost every day now. Some guy was sent back home because a booby trap had blown up on him. And it was about then I started looking for booby traps to step on, taking all sorts of crazy chances, trying to forget about the rain and the cold and the dead children and the corporal. I would go off alone sometimes on patrol looking for the traps, hoping I'd get blown up enough to be sent home, but not enough to get killed. It was a rough kind of game to play. I remember walking along, knowing goddamn well exactly what I was doing, just waiting for those metal splinters to go bursting up into my testicles, sending me home a wounded hero. That was the only way I was getting out of this place. I took more chances than ever before, daydreaming as I strolled through the minefields, thinking of the time I saw a guy named Johnny Temple play in Ebbets Field or the time Duke Snyder struck out and tossed that old bat of his up in the air when the umpire threw him out of the game.

One morning the battalion was blown almost completely apart by an artillery attack. We had been out on patrol most of the night lying in the rain. We weren't even awake when the first couple of rounds began to pound in all around us. There was a whistle, then a cracking explosion. They had us right on target. We all ran for our lives, trying to make it to the bunker we had dug for ourselves. I was still half-asleep and not quite conscious of what was happening to me. All I remember was that I had to get to the bunker. Finally, after what seemed a long time, we all crawled down into the sandbags. We huddled together like children and I heard myself saying "Oh God please God I want to live." Artillery rounds kept crashing in and there was a tremendous explosion in the tent right next to ours. I wondered if anyone had been in it. I continued to pray with all the strength in me that I wouldn't be killed.

When the barrage finally lifted we all looked at each other feeling a little embarrassed for acting so frightened and praying behind the sandbags. Outside the bunker there was a sharp smell of gunpowder and people were beginning to move. I grabbed my green medical bag and told the rest of the men to stay in the bunker and I went out into the sand looking for anyone who was wounded. The first thing I saw was our tent all blown to shit. Big chunks of shrapnel had torn

gaping holes through the corrugated tin roof and
slashed through the tent like the thin stabs of a
knife. We had been hit by almost 150 rounds in
only a few minutes. Everyone was walking around
in a daze.

There were a bunch of men over at the motor
pool kneeling around someone on the ground. I
ran over there as fast as I could, my dog tags
jangling around my neck. They were kneeling
around a guy I knew pretty well. Mac.

I looked down and saw that he was dead. His
neck was almost off and his right arm had been
severed. He had hundreds of silver holes in his
face and chest, looking like little puncture points.
MacCarthy was dead, bleeding in the sand, his
dark blue Boston eyes open and staring up at the
sky. I had just seen him the morning before on
the chow line after we had come in from patrol.
He had smiled at me and told me how everything
was down at the motor pool. But now he was dead
and I picked up my bag and walked back to the
bunker, thinking how MacCarthy had just looked
like a thing, a mannequin. *The dead, he thought,
looked kind of funny in a way, kind of very ridiculous*. I felt almost like laughing and when I came
up to the bunker there was the short kid from
New Jersey who was taking pictures of the de-
molished tent. He was taking pictures with a little
camera with the care and precision of a guy who
should be shooting some pretty trees back home.
I could see that a lot of the men were laughing
and joking now, laughing and joking about the

same thing. *It was like the boy scouts, like the boy scouts getting all chopped up in their pajamas while having a nightmare.*

Another crowd had gathered around a trench. It was hard to tell what had happened there, how many bodies there were. Maybe three all mangled together in a heap, a bunch of arms and legs. There was a smell of gunpowder and blood mixed with burning flesh. One of the heads was completely severed, chopped off, with the exception of a strand of muscle—that was the only thing that continued to connect the head to the stinking corpse. There was nothing any of us could do but pick up the pieces. They seemed very cold and gray and someone in back of me was taking pictures. I fished around for identification in one corpse's dead back pocket and found a wallet. It was Sergeant Bo, one of my friends. He was the supply sergeant and had a wife somewhere. He was sort of the Sergeant Bilko of the battalion. He never went on patrol and had the most comfortable quarters of anyone, with a rug and a desk and a picture of his pretty wife. He had a very young face and now he was in that hole, mangled in that hole, stinking with the others.

The lieutenant came by and ordered the men to put the pieces on a stretcher. Sergeant Bo was my friend and now he was dead. They were going to put him in a plastic bag. They were going to do that with the pieces just like they were going to do with MacCarthy and like they'd done with the corporal from Georgia whom I'd killed the month before. Out by the command bunker they had all the dead lined up in a neat long line. They were all stripped of their clothes and staring up at the sky. Bo and Mac were there with a lot of others I hadn't seen before. About eleven men had been killed in the attack.

There were scores of wounded. Sergeant Peters had been hit in the eye and Corporal Swanson was lying in the command tent with a large piece of metal still stuck in his head. I went up to him and held his hand, telling him everything was going to be all right. He told me to send a letter right away to his wife in California and tell her what had happened. I promised him I'd do it that night but I never did and I never heard from him again.

The men were beginning to relax a little more now. Everyone was smoking cigarettes and feeling a little closer to everyone else. Maybe, I thought, the men would stop talking about me behind my back now. Maybe with all that blown-away flesh the killing of the corporal from Georgia wouldn't mean that much anymore.

He was just another body, he thought, just like the rest of them, the ones who had all been blown to pieces. For some crazy reason he began feeling a lot better about everything. The more the better, he thought, the more that looked like the corporal the better. Maybe, he thought, they would get confused and forget in all the madness that he had murdered the kid from Georgia. Maybe they would understand the mistake of putting the slug in the corporal's neck. He wanted to cry for all his friends who had died that day but he couldn't. He couldn't feel too much anymore.

WE STOPPED GOING out on patrols in the beginning of the new year. We began to take showers every morning and even eat three meals a day again. It seemed like the perfect time to fix up the tent. Michaelson brought in a can of dark oil that we swept all over the wood floor. Even more work was put in on the bunker.

There was news one morning of a big fight a little up north and we began getting restless and edgy. A lieutenant from the battalion had been killed there. I knelt over him with the chaplain when they brought his body in. He was covered with a raincoat. There was a small bullet hole in his forehead and the whole back of his head had been shot out. He was dead like all the rest, and for some reason right then I felt something big was about to happen.

The major called me over and told me to get the men ready to move out. We were going north across the river.

When I got back to the tent, Michaelson told

me he would see me in heaven after today. He was to die that afternoon. Every one of us seemed to have a funny feeling. I kept thinking over and over that I was going to get hit—that nothing would be quite the same after this day.

We went to get some chow and I remember the major yelled at me for not putting helmets on the men. We'd never used them in the past and I couldn't understand why on this day the major wanted us to wear helmets and flak jackets. We had to walk all the way back to our tents and put the stuff on. We felt like supermen in the cumbersome jackets as we got into the truck that took us to the southern bank of the river. We all got out and waited for a while and then a small boat took us to the other side, where everybody else was getting ready to sweep up north to where the lieutenant's squad had been wiped out.

I remember moving along the beach beside the ocean later. There were sand dunes that reminded me of home and lots of scrub pine trees. The men were in a very sloppy formation. It seemed everyone was carrying far too much equipment. The sky was clear and the Vietnamese were walking and fishing. Except for the noise of the tanks and Amtracs that were moving slowly along with us, it seemed like a Sunday stroll with everyone dressed up in costume. It was hard to remember that at any moment the whole thing might bust wide open and you might get killed like all the other dead losers. There was that salt air that smelled so familiar.

Then the whole procession suddenly came to a

stop and we were told to go back. There was
something happening in the village on the north
bank of the river. A big fight was going on and
the Popular Forces were pinned down and in lots
of trouble. I ran up to the captain who had given
the order and asked him was he sure we weren't
supposed to continue going up north. The men
didn't want to go back, I said. Was it the major
who had given the order? I asked. The captain
said he'd try to get confirmation. I waited with the
Amtrac engines roaring in my ears while he
radioed the rear. When he got off the radio, he
told me the major had changed his mind. The
scouts would now lead the attack into the village.

I climbed on one of the Amtracs to talk to the
men. They seemed very quiet. They had the
same feeling I did that it was all about to come
down, that this walk in the sand might be the last
one for all of us.

There was going to be some kind of crazy tacti-
cal maneuver where we were going to march
west along the bank of the river and make a direct
assault on the village after crossing the razorback,
which was the biggest sand dune in the area. A
group of us would dismount from one of the
Amtracs and lead the primary assault and the
other two Amtracs would sweep from north to
south through the graveyard and attack from
another flank. It all sounded so crazy and simple.
I kept trying to get my thoughts together, trying
to think how much I wanted to prove to myself
that I was a brave man, a good marine. No matter
what happened out there, I thought to myself, I

could never retreat. I had to be courageous. Here was my chance to win a medal, here was my chance to fight against the real enemy, to make up for everything that had happened.

This was it, he thought, everything he had been praying for, the whole thing up for grabs.

There were ten of them walking toward the village, and he felt the rosary beads in his top pocket and knew that the little black Bible they had given them all on the planes coming in was in his other pocket too. The other men were getting off the 'tracs in the graveyard. He could see the heat still coming up from the big engines and the men looked real small in the distance, like little toy soldiers jumping off tanks. He looked to the left and they were all there, it was a perfect line. He had trained the scouts well and everything looked good. There was a big pagoda up ahead and a long trench full of Popular Forces. There wasn't any firing going on and he asked the commander of the Viet unit to help him in the assault that was about to take place. The Viet officer said they were staying put and none of them was even going to think about attacking the village. He was angry as he moved the scouts over the top of the long trench line. They're a bunch of fucking cowards, he thought. "Look at them!" he shouted to the scouts. "They're sitting out the war in that trench like a bunch of babies."

"Let's go!" he said. And now they began to move into a wide and open area. They were ten men armed to the teeth, walking in a sweeping line toward the village. It was beautiful, just like the movies.

The firing first started in the graveyard. There were loud cracks, and then the whole thing sounded like someone had set off a whole string of fireworks. He could hear the mortars popping out, crashing like cymbals when they landed on top of the 'tracs. The whole graveyard was being raked by mortars and heavy machine-gun fire coming out of the village.

I remember we all sort of stopped and watched for a moment. Then all of a sudden the cracks were blasting all around our heads and everybody was running all over the place. We started firing back with full automatics. I emptied a whole clip into the pagoda and the village. I was yelling to the men. I kept telling them to hold their ground and keep firing, though no one knew what we were firing at. I looked to my left flank and all the men were gone. They had run away, all run away to the trees near the river, and I yelled and cursed at them to come back but nobody came. I kept emptying everything I had into the village, blasting holes through the pagoda and ripping bullets into the tree line. There was someone to my right lying on the ground still firing.

I had started walking toward the village when the first bullet hit me. There was a sound like firecrackers going off all around my feet. Then a real loud crack and my leg went numb below the knee. I looked down at my foot and there was blood at the back of it. The bullet had come through the front and blew out nearly the whole of my heel.

I had been shot. The war had finally caught up with my body. I felt good inside. Finally the war was with me and I had been shot by the enemy. I was getting out of the war and I was going to be a hero. I kept firing my rifle into the tree line and boldly, with my new wound, moved closer to the village, daring them to hit me again. For a moment I felt like running back to the rear with my new million-dollar wound but I decided to keep fighting out in the open. A great surge of strength went through me as I yelled for the other men to come out from the trees and join me. I was limping now and the foot was beginning to hurt so much, I finally lay down in almost a kneeling position, still firing into the village, still unable to see anyone. I seemed to be the only one left firing a rifle. Someone came up from behind me, took off my boot and began to bandage my foot. The whole thing was incredibly stupid, we were sitting ducks, but he bandaged my foot and then he took off back into the tree line.

For a few seconds it was silent. I lay down prone and waited for the next bullet to hit me. It was only a matter of time, I thought. I wasn't retreating, I wasn't going back, I was lying right there and blasting everything I had into the pagoda. The rifle was full of sand and it was jamming. I had to pull the bolt back now each time trying to get a round into the chamber. It was impossible and I started to get up and a loud crack went off next to my right ear as a thirty-caliber slug tore through my right shoulder, blasted through my lung, and smashed my spinal cord to pieces.

I felt that everything from my chest down was completely gone. I waited to die. I threw my hand back and felt my legs still there. I couldn't feel them but they were still there. I was still alive. And for some reason I started believing, I started believing I might not die, I might make it out of there and live and feel and go back home again. I could hardly breathe and was taking short little sucks with the one lung I had left. The blood was rolling off my flak jacket from the hole in my shoulder and I couldn't feel the pain in my foot anymore, I couldn't even feel my body. I was frightened to death. I didn't think about praying, all I could feel was cheated.

All I could feel was the worthlessness of dying right here in this place at this moment for nothing.

THE BACK YARD, that was the place to be, it was where all the plans for the future, the trips to Africa, the romances with young high-school girls, it was where all those wonderful things took place. Remember the hula hoop, everyone including my mother doing it and my sister, yes my sister, teaching me the twist in the basement. Then out on the basketball court with all the young fine-looking girls watching. Then back on the fence for a walk around the whole back yard. Up there! Can you see me balancing like Houdini? Can you see me hiding in a box, in a submarine, on a jet? Can you see me flying a kite, making a model, breeching a stream?

It was all sort of easy, it had all come and gone, the snowstorms, the street lamps telling us there was no school at midnight, the couch, the heater with all of us rolled up beside it in the thick blankets, the dogs, it was lovely. Getting nailed at home plate, studying the cub scout handbook, tying knots, playing Ping-Pong, reading National

Geographic. *Mickey Mantle was my hero and Joan Marfe was the girl I liked best. It all ended with a bang and it was lovely.*

There was a song called "Runaway" by a guy named Dell Shannon playing one Saturday at the baseball field. I remember it was a beautiful spring day and we were young back then and really alive and the air smelled fresh. This song was playing and I really got into it and was hitting baseballs and feeling like I could live forever.

It was all sort of easy.
It had all come and gone.